NEW MEXICO
AND THE
CIVIL WAR

NEW MEXICO
AND THE
CIVIL WAR

DR. WALTER EARL PITTMAN

Charleston   London

THE
History
PRESS

Published by The History Press
Charleston, SC 29403
www.historypress.net

First published 2011
Second printing 2011

Manufactured in the United States

ISBN 978.1.60949.137.6

Library of Congress Cataloging-in-Publication Data

Pittman, Walter E.
New Mexico and the Civil War / Walter Earl Pittman.
p. cm.
ISBN 978-1-60949-137-6
1. New Mexico--History--Civil War, 1861-1865. I. Title.
E522.P48 2011
978.9'04--dc22
2011014425

Contents

Chapter 1

The New Mexico Territory in 1861

The New Mexico Territory in 1861, comprising the later states of Arizona and New Mexico, was a huge, sparsely populated region, far removed from any other American population center. In an area larger than the Deep South, it recorded only 93,516 inhabitants, mostly poor Hispano farmers and civilized Pueblo Indians living along the rivers, where water was available for agriculture. Most people lived near the Rio Grande, from Socorro north into Colorado. Around them was wilderness in all directions, peopled by large, warlike tribes who had depredated the settlers for centuries. There were Apaches to the south, Navajos to the west and Utes in the north, and on the Plains to the east roamed the bands of Comanches, Jicarilla Apaches and Kiowas.

Santa Fe, the capital city and largest town, was a dusty adobe village of 4,600 souls. Mesilla, at the southern end of the territory, was even more isolated and primitive and had only 2,600 inhabitants. Mesilla and the lower Rio Grande settlements were separated from the main centers of population, Albuquerque and Santa Fe, by some two hundred miles of inhospitable wilderness, including the dread "Jornada del Muerto" (Journey of Death), a dangerous desert passage. To the west was the large and even wilder land acquired from Mexico in the Gadsden Purchase. Only 2,421 people, civilized enough to be enumerated by the census taken, lived there. As in New Mexico, many of the Anglos were actually soldiers stationed at the numerous forts and camps scattered throughout the region. Most of the remainder lived in Tucson, in the mining center at Tubac near the Mexican border or in small farming or mining communities that were beginning to develop around army posts.

Most of the population of the territory (not counting the Indians) were Hispanic and of Mexican origin. Almost all had some degree of Indian ancestry. As a result of centuries of extreme isolation, most New Mexicans had little knowledge and even less interest in events in the larger world. The small number (two hundred families) of educated upper-class New Mexicans (the "ricos" or "rich") looked to Mexico and Missouri for social, cultural and religious fashions. These wealthy New Mexicans—like the Armijo brothers, rich merchants who were the sons of the last Mexican governor of New Mexico, and Miguel A. Otero, the territory's representative to the U.S. Congress—were strongly pro-Southern in their political outlook. Indian slavery and debt peonage were widespread in New Mexico. Miguel A. Otero actively sought to align New Mexico with the South and pushed through a stringent slave code for the territory in 1859, although there were only a handful of black slaves in the immense territory. These Hispano grandees had tremendous influence among the poorer classes. Their leadership, as well as lingering resentments resulting from annexation of the territory in 1847 as a result of the Mexican-American War, created some lukewarm support for the soldiers of the Confederacy among the natives. It would not last, though.

In the fourteen years during which the United States had controlled the Southwest after taking it from Mexico, there had been constant warfare with the Navajos and Apaches. The U.S. Army was tasked to prevent the wild tribes from raiding Anglo and Hispano settlers, the civilized Pueblo tribes and the Mexicans in north Mexico, their primary source of livelihood. Historically, they made their living raiding the civilized tribes and settlers.

The almost endless campaigning by seriously undermanned military forces was centered on a string of forts stretching from San Antonio to Yuma, Arizona, and from Fort Union in northern New Mexico to Fort Buchanan in southern Arizona. Other forts were scattered in the Navajo country, where a larger war was being fought. Apache violence flared in 1860 and 1861, as attacks on white settlers and travelers increased in frequency, severity and duration.

There were several reasons for this outburst of Indian violence. When the hostilities of the Civil War commenced in 1861, the United States government quickly moved to concentrate its available military forces where they were needed most, in the East, and abandon the (now) less critical Indian campaigns in the West. In New Mexico and Arizona, this meant abandoning (and burning) the far-flung outposts like Forts Buchanan, Breckinridge, McLane and so on to allow the Regular forces stationed there to march east to join the big war. The small remaining Regular forces were to be concentrated at Santa Fe, Fort Union and Fort Craig. In reality, because of the Confederate invasion and the Indian attacks, far fewer troops could be sent east than the government had planned. Watching from their wilderness outposts, the hostile Indians saw the withdrawal of the troops as a victory, and

Forts of New Mexico, 1861.

recognizing the relative weakness of the army, they were quick to strike the exposed settlements.

Stationed at the army forts scattered across the New Mexico Territory's plains, deserts and mountains were about 2,600 men in mid-1861. Many of these marched east, but most remained and were reinforced with newly raised volunteer units from New Mexico and Colorado. By the end of 1861, 5,646 Union soldiers were under arms, and by mid-1862, there were more than 7,000. Their commander was Colonel E.R.S. Canby, a cautious, realistic and prudent infantryman who would succeed in destroying a Confederate army without winning a battle. In the process, he acquired a reputation as a chivalric and gentlemanly warrior unmatched by any other Union officer. He rose to command when his two superior officers in the Department of New Mexico resigned to join the Confederacy. One, Colonel Henry H.H. Sibley, would soon return to New Mexico at the head of an invading army of Texans.

Chapter 2

High Times for Dixie

When General Henry Sibley went to Richmond to offer his services to the Confederacy, he left behind him in New Mexico weak and demoralized Union forces. Scattered in small posts across the barren landscape, the troops had not been paid for months; received poor and inadequate rations, clothing and equipment; and were dispirited by the defections of their officers to the Confederacy. Observing this as he traveled south and east from Fort Union to San Antonio, Henry Sibley began to dream a big dream. New Mexico was weakly held, he believed; it could be seized almost without a struggle. And New Mexico was the key to the whole Southwest: the gold fields of Colorado, Arizona and sparsely populated northern Mexico—and then California. It was the dream of a Confederate empire stretching from sea to sea that Sibley took with him to Richmond to lay before his old friend, Jefferson Davis. It could be done, Sibley believed, almost without cost. The Rebels could live on captured supplies stockpiled in the numerous forts. Sibley returned to Texas in July 1861, with a commission as brigadier general and the authority to raise an army to invade New Mexico.

Colonel Canby—who, ironically, was fated a decade later to become the highest-ranking army officer ever killed by Indians—faced tremendous problems. In July 1861, the U.S. War Department reversed the plans to abandon New Mexico and Arizona. However, nearly half of the Regulars were still sent east, and Canby got very little support in manpower, money or supplies to help him prepare for the coming invasion. For soldiers, he had to rely on the native New Mexicans to man volunteer and militia regiments. Canby did not regard the New Mexican soldiers as effective or reliable. In fact, they proved to be even worse in combat than he had feared. Unwilling to risk the native troops—about half of his strength on the field of battle—Canby devised a strategy to avoid this.

Canby knew, as Sibley apparently didn't, that no army can subsist on the barren New Mexico countryside. And so he took energetic measures to ensure that the invaders wouldn't be able to live off captured stores, either. Stockpiles of supplies were moved from the exposed forts (Bliss, Stanton, McLane and Fillmore) or were destroyed. The Arizona forts were abandoned, as well as Forts McLane and Bliss, and preparations were made to abandon and destroy Forts Fillmore and Stanton. The troops in these forts were to be gathered either at Fort Craig in the south

Fort Union. *Courtesy of Mike Werve.*

or Fort Union in the north. Fort Union was the military key to New Mexico, situated near the western end of the Santa Fe Trail, it controlled the long logistical lifeline of the territory, stretching back more than one thousand miles to the Missouri River. Fort Craig sat athwart any invasion from the south and would have to be taken before invaders could move into the heart of New Mexico. Or, at least, so Canby thought. Hurriedly, Canby had Fort Union rebuilt with a more defensible siting and design, and he expanded and strengthened Fort Craig.

Events moved faster in the New Mexico Territory than they did in the East. The population in the southern part of the territory had long been thoroughly alienated from the Santa Fe government over its failure to protect them from Indians and saw hope in the new Confederacy. In the southern part of the territory, a call went out for a constitutional convention to meet in March 1861 in Mesilla. It adopted a territorial constitution and sent representatives to Richmond seeking acceptance of the "Territory of Arizona" by the Confederate Congress. This comprised the southern halves of modern Arizona and New Mexico up to 36°, 30'N. It eventually became the Confederate Territory of Arizona and, like the Indian Territory, had representation in the Confederate Congress. However, by then Confederate Arizona was a government in exile in Texas.

The Confederate government of Arizona quickly authorized the creation of several companies of volunteer irregular cavalry for protection from Indians and Yankees. The first of these, the San Elizario (Spy) Company, numbered about 40 men and already had been in existence since February 1861. Together, these units totaled 105 men at their greatest. At Fort Fillmore alone were 700 Federal troops in the heart of the new Confederate Territory of Arizona. Worried about the danger this garrison posed to the military supplies stockpiled at abandoned Fort Bliss, the leaders of the new Rebel territory appealed to their compatriots in Texas. In response, a battalion of the Second Texas Mounted Volunteers (TMV) under Lieutenant Colonel John Baylor was hurried westward from San Antonio.

Baylor arrived at Fort Bliss on July 13, 1861, at the head of six small companies, totaling 256 men. They were untrained and armed mostly with old shotguns brought from home. It was a miniscule force to conquer an empire, but the audacious Baylor gave it a good try. Even before he had arrived, the San Elizario Company had driven off more than two hundred horses and mules from Fort Fillmore. A second raid in late July netted eighty-five cavalry horses and twenty-six mules. Apache raiders regularly drove off even more. These losses seriously crippled the Union garrison's ability to either fight or run.

The ever daring Baylor moved almost immediately against Fort Fillmore, although the well-armed Federals outnumbered him two to one, seven hundred men of the Seventh Infantry and four companies of Regular cavalry to his three hundred amateur warriors. An attempted surprise nighttime attack on the fort on July 24 was foiled when a deserter slipped across the Rio Grande to warn the garrison. Undeterred, Baylor simply marched on past the fort on an unguarded road to seize Mesilla. He and his men received an enthusiastic welcome from the pro-Southern population, many of whom joined Baylor's force. Major Isaac Lynde, the aging Federal commander of Fort Fillmore, seemed stunned by this development and did nothing for a time.

When Lynde finally marched from Fort Fillmore toward Mesilla on July 25, 1861, he took with him about 380 of his 700 troops. These were U.S. Regulars, well equipped and well trained. Lynde advanced with six companies of his own Seventh Infantry and two companies of cavalry from the Regiment of Mounted Riflemen, RMR, covered by two twelve-pound mountain howitzers. To oppose them, Baylor had about 300 men, including the San Elizario Company and some civilian volunteers. Most were armed with old shotguns and other poor weapons. Baylor deployed his men behind adobe walls and on the roofs of buildings along the eastern side of the village. Most New Mexico buildings were built of adobe—thick walled (twenty inches), with flat roofs and surrounded by low adobe walls. Adobe has an amazing ability to absorb bullets and projectiles, making every house and village a potential impromptu fortification.

Lynde marched his troops to within 300 yards and deployed them in the flat fields in line before sending into the village a flag of truce with a demand that the Rebels surrender. Baylor replied that "we would fight first and surrender afterword." This response seemed to unnerve Lynde again. He hesitated and did nothing for a while. Finally, the Federal howitzers opened a brief bombardment on the town that failed to claim any Confederates but did kill a lot of horses. The Federal cavalry lined up about 250 yards from the village, preparing to charge. Baylor called on the few men with rifles in Gooch Hardeman's Company A, the nearest to the enemy, to try to pick off the officers. In short order, Captain C.H. McNally, commanding the cavalry, was hit three times, but he would eventually recover. Enthusiastically, the other Rebels now began blasting away with their shotguns and revolvers, killing three and wounding six Federals at extreme range for their weapons.

When two of the men serving the artillery pieces were hit, the spirit seemed to flow out of the Union soldiers like air from a pricked balloon. Hurriedly, they abandoned the field, although their losses had been minuscule. The Southerners had only six men wounded. Baylor didn't try to pursue. He recognized that only a portion of Lynde's force was present in front of Mesilla, and believing that the weakly prosecuted attack had been only a feint, he feared that Lynde planned to trap him in the Rio Grande bottom. He gave the Yankee major too much credit. Baylor's scouts soon reported that the Yankees had retreated all the way back to Fort Fillmore. Lynde did not remain long. Fort Fillmore, dominated by high ground, was indefensible—or would have been if Baylor had any heavy artillery. It had already been determined by Union authorities to evacuate the post and concentrate Union forces at Fort Craig, ninety miles to the north on the Rio Grande, and at Fort Stanton, which watched over a possible Pecos River invasion route 120 miles to the northeast. Fort Fillmore was to be held long enough for the Federal troops withdrawing from Arizona to join up with Lynde's command. But after the farce at Mesilla and the loss of his horses, Lynde feared (quite correctly) that the aggressive Baylor would soon attack him and hastened to abandon the fort.

In the early hours of July 27, Lynde set his garrison in motion, retreating northeast toward Fort Stanton, although his well-armed and well-equipped Regulars still outnumbered Baylor's men two to one. The

San Elizario scouts were deployed close around the fort and at daylight discovered and quickly reported to Baylor the Federal movements. The Confederates were able to move into the fort and save most of the buildings and supplies that had been set afire in a half-hearted attempt at destruction. Lynde chose to retreat toward Fort Stanton, which led him away from the Rio Grande and across the desert uplands sloping toward the Organ Mountains to the east. This decision, fatal as it turned out, was made because of his belief that the Confederates had already interdicted the direct route to Fort Craig along the Rio Grande with strong forces. Actually, Thomas Mastin's fifty men of the Arizona Guards were the only Rebels between Lynde and Fort Craig, but they apparently were able to fool him.

The route taken by Fort Fillmore garrison led them across desert uplands, on a day that grew steadily hotter, during an unusually dry season in New Mexico. Little water was brought along by the column, and no effort had been made to check on the condition of the spring at San Augustin Pass, which was the garrison's destination, or of the only other spring along their route before the march began. Both proved to be nearly dry. Lynde was clearly panicked. Later, his officers turned on him, blaming the disaster entirely on him and accusing him of cowardice and/or treason. However, there is no evidence that they opposed his actions at the time. Furthermore, even had Lynde been able to get his command to the San Augustin Springs, it is very difficult to understand how he could have successfully crossed the next barrier, the seventy-mile-wide Tularosa Basin, which was even more arid. The only spring along his path to Fort Stanton was nearly dry at this season. The twenty-mile march to San Augustin should have been within the capability of the Federal troops, but many, perhaps most, of the Regulars had filled their canteens with commissary whiskey at Fort Fillmore rather than destroy it as ordered. The men grew more and more thirsty as the day grew hotter, and they turned to their canteens with disastrous results. The road, which was rough and relatively steep in places, was soon lined with hundreds of soldiers who had collapsed, unable to go farther.

The Federals had actually managed to get a head start on the Confederates, estimated by Baylor at four hours, by leaving before daylight at 1:00 a.m. When daylight came and the San Elizario scouts reported that the fort had been abandoned, Baylor set off in pursuit. He could see the dust raised by Lynde's column heading northeast for San Augustin Pass, the only practical way through the rugged Organ Mountains. Leaving nearly half of his force to secure Fort Fillmore and its badly needed supplies, Baylor headed northeast with 162 men, selected because they had the best horses, trying to head the Federals off at San Augustin Pass. Baylor's men soon began to overtake the Yankee column. Hundreds of soldiers lined the roads, unable to proceed, begging for water. Some were unconscious. Twenty-four were captured asleep at a spring in the mountains, where they had gone seeking water. At first, Baylor's men disarmed the Union soldiers and pressed on, but there were so many that they soon gave up even that. Led by the San Elizario Company in the van, the Rebel horsemen captured the wagon train, the artillery and 108 civilians, soldiers' dependents, before they reached the pass. Union cavalry, assigned as a rear guard, tried to buy time and repeatedly deployed to fight but then turned tail when the Confederates charged. Lynde and his cavalry advance reached San Augustin Springs, which are actually located on the eastern slope of the mountains, only to find them nearly dry. He turned back to rejoin the main body and met San Elizario spies instead, with Baylor close behind. After a futile attempt to form a line of battle, Lynde simply surrendered—700 Regulars to fewer than 200 "long eared, ragged Texans."

For two days, Baylor lingered near the pass, trying to keep his new prisoners alive by rushing water to them or, conversely, moving them to water. The prisoners—comprising eight companies of infantry of the Seventh Infantry Regiment and four of cavalry of the Regiment of Mounted Riflemen—were simply paroled. The Southerners could neither feed nor guard that many men, and so they were sent back to Fort Craig on their sworn oath not to take up arms until exchanged. They were provided with food, wagons and enough guns to protect them from the Indians on their trip.

Some of the Federal cavalrymen who escaped from San Augustin hurried on to Fort Stanton, carrying panic with them. The commander of the four-company post on the Bonita River, Lieutenant Colonel Benjamin

Fort Stanton.

Fort Stanton, 1866.

S. Roberts, had discretionary orders that allowed him to withdraw his garrison to Albuquerque and Fort Craig if he thought that the situation required it. Immediately upon hearing of San Augustin Pass, he hastily abandoned the post, although there was not a Rebel soldier within one hundred miles, and none was coming his direction. On August 2, 1861, the Federals quit the picturesque little fort, abandoning a battery of artillery and setting several small fires that were quickly extinguished by local pro-Southern citizens (aided by a rain shower).

The local men then sent a delegation to Mesilla to ask Baylor to send troops to Fort Stanton to recover the considerable military supplies at the fort and, not so incidentally, protect them and their often substantial properties from the Apaches. In response, Baylor sent sixty-five men of Company D under Captain James Walker. The English-born Walker was a physician who had attended West Point for three years until a mathematics deficiency had changed his career path. Walker's men retrieved most of the supplies left at the fort from the Apaches and local farmers who had looted it. They held the fort for one month and fought Indians twice during their tenure. A four-man patrol on outpost duty at Gallinas Spring, some forty-eight miles northwest of the fort, was surprised by a band of Kiowas through their own carelessness. Only one man survived. On the night of September 8, fifteen men of the company fought a pitched battle to save Placitas (later Lincoln) from Mescalero Apaches, killing five. The company, its mission completed, started back to Mesilla on September 9, 1862. En route they encountered a company of New Mexico troops who surrendered without a fight and were simply disarmed and sent home. The remaining settlers, bereft of protection from the Indians, fled to more civilized areas. For a year, the ruined fort and the Bonita Valley would remain empty except for the Apaches and an occasional scouting party.

Chapter 3

The Army of New Mexico

By the time General Sibley returned to Texas to recruit his "Army of New Mexico," it was already too late. To have a chance of success, Sibley's army had to reach New Mexico before the Union defenders had time to organize, as well as before winter, when it would be impossible to forage off the countryside. Sibley believed, and he told President Jefferson Davis, that the campaign would be self-sustaining from captures. It might have been true if they had reached New Mexico in August as Sibley had planned, but it was late January 1862 before the last troops arrived. It was far too late. It was not all Sibley's fault, although he was a thoroughly impractical dreamer. He also eventually came to be viewed by his own men as a drunk and a coward, thoughtless of their health or lives.

In Texas, recruiting early in the war had already taken many of the available men to eastern battlefields, and with them went most of the uniforms, guns and artillery available in Texas. Sibley had no money to buy more even if he had found a supply. The troops he could gather were armed with whatever weapons could be found, usually shotguns brought from home, as were their uniforms. Sibley created two four-gun batteries of light field artillery, and Baylor had captured seven more light guns. The Rebels had no heavy artillery, but they couldn't have taken big guns seven hundred miles across the desert anyway. The little Army of New Mexico (it was actually the size of a brigade) was well mounted,

General H.H. Sibley, CSA.
Courtesy of the Library of Congress.

at least at first, with plenty of good horses mostly brought from home by the soldiers. Finally despairing of ever filling out his regiments with recruits or equipping them, Sibley set the units that were more or less ready into motion west on October 23, 1861. There were the Fourth and Fifth TMV, and later the incomplete Seventh TMV, the size of a battalion, would follow. At its greatest strength, the Army of New Mexico numbered 3,200 men, including Baylor's battalion and locally raised irregular units.

The journey westward was long and difficult. The trek began in October, but the last units did not arrive until late January 1862. Widely separated water holes of small capacity supplied a lifeline through the desert. Units had to march in small increments, widely separated, to avoid exhausting the water supply. Around them hovered the Mescalero Apaches, eager to snap up livestock or unwary Texans. Sibley provided barely enough food even for the men to reach the Rio Grande, and there was little for them when they got there. The available supplies had been exhausted by Baylor's men, and Sibley lacked hard money to buy more. There was plenty of food available nearby in Mexico, but not for Confederate money. Disease also struck the Texans hard, especially pneumonia and measles. Some companies altogether had 15 percent of their men die from measles. It was an army already in serious trouble before it even reached New Mexico.

After taking Mesilla and Fort Fillmore, Colonel John Baylor moved to establish a government for the Confederacy's most distant province. On August 1, 1861, he issued a proclamation creating the Confederate Territory of Arizona with himself as governor. The Confederate Congress accepted the territory on February 14, 1862. Baylor also redefined the border of the new Rebel territory, extending it northward to 36°, 30'N, west to the Colorado River and south to the mouth of that river. A large portion of Mexican territory was, therefore, included in Baylor's boundaries. Baylor appointed several Hispanos to high governmental posts, hoping to win the allegiance of what was the majority of the population. He understood that the Confederates would need their support. With the arrival of Sibley's larger Confederate forces at the end of the year, commanded by officers lacking Baylor's commitment to good relations, conditions soon deteriorated to open enmity between the Confederates, all Texans, and the native New Mexicans.

After the disaster at San Augustin, Union forces were content to wait in their forts for something else to happen. Despite outnumbering Baylor's little force tenfold, Canby remained passive. The Confederates, very conscious of their inferiority, expected Canby to move against them before they could be reinforced. They made plans for such a contingency based on the "skedaddle" to El Paso or across the border into Mexico. Baylor's secret agents reported about November 20 that Canby was ready to move south with a force six times the Rebel strength. Hurriedly, the military and civilian residents fled south carrying what they could of their possessions and supplies and burying or destroying the remainder. But nothing happened.

The Union soldiers remained in their tents and barracks, and the embarrassed Southerners eventually returned to Mesilla. Baylor was the most embarrassed of all. He had sent several urgent messages to the troops coming from San Antonio: "Hurry up if you want a fight." But no fight occurred. One of those who blamed Baylor for the comedy was the aggressive editor of the *Mesilla Times*, Robert Kelly, who had published several of Baylor's alarming reports. He had fled south like so many of the Southerners in Mesilla, burying his little press in the desert. Kelly now blamed Baylor for the whole fiasco and viciously crucified him in every issue of the *Mesilla Times*. Notoriously thin-skinned and proud, Baylor fumed and raged, demanding a retraction and an apology. Kelly refused. He had a grievance against Baylor dating from a failed contract bid to supply feed to Baylor's force and hoped to force him into a duel. Kelly was an expert pistol shot. Finally, on the morning of December 12, 1861, as Kelly walked past Baylor's office on the plaza at Mesilla, Baylor

Bredett C. Murray, 1872, Brigand and editor of the *Mesilla Times*. *Courtesy of Bredett C. Thomas.*

waylaid him. Again he demanded an apology from the editor, and when he refused, Baylor knocked him to the ground with a rifle he took from a soldier. They scuffled, and Baylor shot the editor through the head, mortally wounding him, when he tried to draw a knife. Frank Higgins and Bredett C. Murray, who took over the paper, quickly announced their intention to steer clear of any further controversy, a pledge they scrupulously kept. Although cleared of charges by a court made up of his own officers, Baylor's reputation never recovered.

Baylor failed to trap the Federal troops retreating from Arizona. Orders from Washington to abandon the Arizona forts and send most of the Regulars back to the "states," concentrating the remainder at Forts Fillmore and Craig, had sparked a flurry of activity. Every available wagon and team in Arizona was hired but could carry only a fraction of the stockpiled military stores. The remainder was first offered for public sale and then mostly given away to Indians and loyal citizens or destroyed. The column of 250 men, forty wagons, two six-pound artillery pieces and an eight-wagon train of civilians left Fort Breckenridge on July 30 heading for the Rio Grande and Fort Fillmore, which was already in Confederate hands, unknown to them. The column, commanded by Captain Isaiah Moore, moved slowly across country, dogged by the heat, lack of water and widespread sickness among the men. They managed to slip by the Confederates moving to intercept them after they were warned by Vergil Massie of Baylor's intention. Destroying their wagons and guns, they made their way to Fort Craig in a desperate nighttime march. Actually, they were better armed and about equal in numbers to the Rebels. Baylor had put a big "scare" into the Yankees, and for six months General Canby apprehensively, and passively, eyed the little Rebel force but did nothing.

In the 120-mile-long gap between the Confederates at Mesilla and Yankees at Fort Craig, scouts from each side tangled frequently. On August 20, 1861, Captain Santiago (James) Hubble led his company of New Mexico Volunteers, reinforced with twenty Regular cavalrymen, south to raid the Rebel horse herd. They were ambushed by the San Elizario Company under Captain Bethel Coopwood. Most of Hubble's men deserted, and he was forced to surrender the remainder. The only

Confederate casualty was the diminutive Cuban, Enrique D'Hamel, whose arm was hit by a spent bullet. The minor wound became infected, and D'Hamel lapsed into a coma, was pronounced dead and was prepared for burial at Fort Fillmore hospital. A drunken comrade, refusing to accept the medical ruling, sat on his bed for several days with loaded pistols to prevent his burial, until he regained consciousness and, eventually, his health.

A more serious clash of the scouts occurred on September 25, when Coopwood's San Elizario Company, reinforced up to 114 men with some of Baylor's men, struck Captain John Mink's company of 100 New Mexico troops at Alamosa, thirty-five miles south of Fort Craig. Coopwood, who apparently had advance knowledge of Mink's plans, struck at 2:00 a.m. The surprised volunteers took refuge in the adobe buildings of the village and fought back. Throughout the night, Mink's force withered away, as the volunteers deserted and fled across the river. Mink had only ten men left at dawn and surrendered. Coopwood leisurely headed back south, with his loot and three prisoners. The New Mexico troops were simply disarmed and paroled.

The Rebels camped on the river at the "E Company Grove" that night. They weren't anticipating pursuit. Up to now, Union troops had reacted only with passivity. However, Captain R.M. Morris and three companies (180 men) of the Regiment of Mounted Riflemen made a forced eighty-mile march and fell on the surprised Rebels just as they were cooking breakfast. Coopwood reported, "None of ordinary ceremonies of attack were performed. These being no misunderstanding, we at once commenced business." Morris failed to exploit his advantages of numbers (180 to 114), surprise, longer-range weapons or position. With his larger numbers, Morris was able to overlap the Rebels on both flanks and subject them to crossfire, but he failed to attack. A desultory, long-range exchange of gunfire lasted for four hours, until Morris decided that his ammunition was running low and returned to Fort Craig. The Rebels were amazed but delighted at his retreat. They had lost two men and thirty horses (killed). Among the wounded was Lieutenant Metiaze Medina, a New Mexico Volunteer prisoner from Mink's command who was wounded through the upper leg by his own men.

Baylor's scouts probably found that fighting Yankees was preferable to fighting the ever hostile Apaches. On August 11, Lieutenant Reuban E. Mays and eleven men were ambushed and killed near Fort Davis. They had recovered some one hundred head of stolen horses and were returning to the fort. Mays impetuously charged into the ambush, although he had been warned by his guide. Farther west in modern Arizona, a wagon train (the Ake train) of wealthy settlers escaping from Arizona was ambushed at Cooke Canyon. Pinned down by more than one hundred Apaches, the party finally escaped by abandoning the livestock and members' rich belongings. Five miles away, they met Captain Tom Mastin and his Arizona Guards (thirty men), a Rebel scout company raised around the Pinos Altos Mines. Mastin understood that the Apaches would simply scatter if he were to chase after them. Instead, he anticipated where they were headed, got ahead of them and set up his own ambush in the Florida Mountains. Eighty warriors blundered into the trap, nine were killed and about half of the lost livestock was recovered. It was a small revenge.

These were even worse signs of things to come. The Ake train had been attacked by Apaches from several different tribes—Chiricahuas, Mimbres, Warm Springs and so on—who rarely had contact. Something was bringing them together. That something was the huge (six feet, four inches tall) Mimbreño chief, Mangas Coloradas, who was determined to rid himself of the Pinos Altos mining camp, located in the heart of the Mimbres Apache homeland. The attack came at dawn on September 27, 1861, when three hundred Apaches struck with surprise. The camp, scattered along the ravines and gullies, was almost overrun. Several cabins held out as strong points and provided defensive crossfire. Finally, a small cannon was pulled out of Roy and Sam Bean's store filled with every kind of metal available and loosed upon the Apaches. "You bet it made them scatter," Arizona Guard Hank Smith remembered. The miners then bravely counterattacked, scattering the Apaches for good. In the aftermath, most of the miners, shocked at the size and persistence of the Apache attacks, fled the Gila Mountains. Actually, the Apaches, stung by their losses, would never mount another large-scale attack.

At this stage of the campaign, the Confederate scouts seem to have gotten the best of the war between the forts. By December 1862, Rebel horsemen operated close around Fort Craig, probing its defenses "nightly and sometimes as often as three or four times in a single night." Part of the beef herd (two hundred animals) was driven off. Supply trains could only reach the fort under heavy guard, and rations had to be cut. Fort Craig was almost in a state of siege before Sibley's army arrived. Some Confederate scouts also operated regularly around Fort Union and Anton Chico, between Santa Fe and Fort Union, two hundred miles behind Union lines. Others reached southern Colorado, four hundred miles away, to make contact with Confederate guerrillas there.

As the campaign progressed, Union scouts, who were primarily native New Mexicans, proved increasingly valuable to General Canby. Both sides seem to have had excellent intelligence on the other side's strength, location, armament and condition of their forces. The most famous and the most capable of the Union scout companies was the company of New Mexico Volunteers, raised and commanded by Captain James "Paddy" Graydon, a former dragoon and saloonkeeper from Arizona. Graydon's men were skilled at penetrating Confederate New Mexico undetected and harassing the Rebel lines of communications. These were some lapses, as when Graydon reported that two companies of Confederate blacks had marched through Franklin (El Paso). Paddy also had a drinking problem. His men earned a well-deserved reputation for rapine, drunkenness and looting but performed capably in the field.

Soon after Sibley's arrival in New Mexico, the general created a highly secret "spy" company. Quickly labeled the "Brigands" by the other Rebels, they were also known as the "Santa Fe Gamblers," because their captain, John G. Phillips, was a gambler who owned the premier hotel/gambling establishment in Santa Fe, the Exchange Hotel, and had recruited many of his friends. Between thirty-seven and fifty-three men served as Brigands, and they proved to be the most formidable fighters in Sibley's army. About half of the Brigands were Northerners or foreign born. At the war's end in Texas, they would be among the last diehard Confederates who refused to surrender and fled to Mexico in an effort to continue the war. At the same time the Brigands were created, Baylor created another special unit, Company A, that was destined to carry the war to its westernmost limits.

Sibley's grandly styled Army of New Mexico began arriving at Franklin (El Paso) on November 9, 1861. Lead elements of the Fourth TMV, commanded by Major Henry Raguet, were followed by the rest of the regiment under Colonel James Riley. Colonel Tom Green followed with the Fifth TMV at staggered intervals. Finally, seven companies of the incomplete Seventh TMV, under Lieutenant Colonel John S. Sutton, headed out of San Antonio on November 28, and three more companies followed on December 18, reaching Fort Thorn in early February 1862. General Sibley and his staff arrived at Fort Bliss on December 13, 1861.

Chapter 4

Valverde

By this point, Sibley should have realized that his scheme of having his army live off captured stores while it conquered a western empire was no longer possible—if it ever had been. His indifference to logistical realities is usually attributed to his romanticism or alcoholism—or both. Either Sibley turned to the bottle to ease the chronic pain of kidney disease, or the bottle caused his problem. Either way, he was incapacitated during every combat the Rebel army fought, leaving the command to others. Indifferent to his men's welfare, and that of their horses that were their personal property, he earned the cordial hatred of most by the campaign's end.

His protagonist, General E.R.S. Canby, was a shrewd, cautious and realistic old soldier. The two men were old friends dating from West Point days. They were rumored to be brothers-in-law but were not. They had served together in the small Regular army, including the Utah campaign in 1858 and several Indian campaigns. Both men fought according to an older, chivalric tradition that ameliorated, in New Mexico, some of the worst horrors of warfare. Both also shared a racially condescending attitude toward New Mexico's native population that partially determined their respective strategies.

Sibley's army was a wasting asset. He could not feed his army or its animals in the lower Rio Grande Valley where they were. He either had to move forward and conquer or starve. By the time the campaign began, the army had less than two weeks of food for the men and even less for

MAP OF THE CAMPAIGN AND OF SIBLEY'S RETREAT.
From *Battles and Leaders of the Civil War.*

Map of the campaign and of Sibley's retreat. From *Battles And Leaders.*

the animals. It was not even enough to retreat safely to San Antonio. The only way was forward.

On February 7, 1862, the van of Sibley's army left old Fort Thorn and marched north along the Rio Grande. Colonel Tom Green and his Fifth TMV led the way. Ahead, Rebel scouts pushed close to the walls of Fort Craig, spreading alarm. By February 12, Green had closed to within twenty miles of Fort Craig, and the opposing scouts regularly reported one another's presence near the Rio Grande. That night, Major Charles Pyron arrived with part of Baylor's command and the three volunteer "spy" or "scout" companies: the San Elizario Company under Captain Bethel Coopwood, the Arizona Rangers under Captain George Frazer and the Brigands. Some of these local volunteers also accompanied each regiment as guides.

The next morning, Green, a much-beloved veteran of the Mexican-American War and former clerk of the Texas Supreme Court, led his force (930 men) north. They encamped about ten miles south of the fort. Soon after their arrival, Rebel scouts met a Union scouting force of two companies under Captain Benjamin Wingate. Both sides reinforced their scouts

Site of old Fort Thorn.

31

and took up strong positions behind arroyo banks in the hope that their opponents would attack. Neither did. Finally, the Federals withdrew to Fort Craig. Facing Canby's deployed force, Green had hurriedly sent messengers south to spur on the troops not already on the way. The men of the Fourth and Seventh TMVs left their camps at midnight in a winter storm and "had to face a north wind with sleet and snow falling so hard as to almost pelt the skin off their faces." Then they had to camp without food or bedding.

Over half of Sibley's supply wagons had been abandoned at Fort Thorn for lack of animals to draw them. The remainder had been loaded preferentially with ammunition and whatever food could be fit in. Left behind were tents, bedding and extra clothes, in a severe winter. The loss of horses and mules was primarily due to malnutrition, which made the animals susceptible to disease. However, there were constant losses to the ever present Apache raiders, who preyed on the herds night after night.

The Confederate Army of New Mexico was now concentrated, and its bibulous commander had to make a decision. Sibley confided his plans to an old friend, Alexander Melvorne Jackson, who served as his assistant adjutant. Jackson, an aristocratic Mississippian, had been the prewar secretary of the territory and understood New Mexico well. Sibley knew that he had to capture supplies for his army in order to survive. But he had no intention, or capability, of directly attacking Fort Craig. He intended to bypass the fort and push up the river to cut off the fort from its supply lines and force Canby out to fight in the open. Failing that, he would presumably starve the garrison out. A Rebel soldier noted perceptively that "Gen. Sibley's idea of cutting our enemy's supplies was a bright one indeed. We had about 3 days rations and the enemy I expect has about 6 months in the Fort." And the Federals were getting more. One of the strange aspects of the New Mexico campaign was Sibley's failure to utilize his superiority in cavalry to interdict the Union line of communication north of Fort Craig. Even as the Rebel army approached, a supply train of seventy wagons reached the fort, topping off the already well-filled magazines.

Early on Sunday morning, February 16, the Rebel army stirred and moved out of its cold camps toward Fort Craig. It was watched by Captain Paddy Graydon's scouts, who soon sent word back to General Canby that the Rebels were coming. To the approaching Rebels the fort appeared to

Fort Craig.

be deserted. Over it hung the ever recognizable Stars and Stripes. Then Sibley's approaching men saw soldiers pouring from the fort to take up position in front of it.

Canby aligned his artillery in the center, except for the heavy twenty-four-pound howitzers, which remained in the fort. The dismounted men deployed on each side of the guns. On the higher ground to the west were most of the cavalry, sited to watch the enemy and prevent a flank movement. The Rebels approached to within two miles of the fort. When this brought no reaction, Tom Green moved them to within one thousand yards of the walls. Still, Canby refused to move his men from the shadows of the comforting walls of Fort Craig. For several hours, the two armies stood watching each other as the day turned colder and it began to snow. Canby tried to goad the Confederates into attacking his strong position by sending two cavalry companies galloping between the lines, with Graydon "turning and wheeling [his horse] like a circus man." There was some firing at extreme range, resulting in one Union soldier killed and another wounded. Finally, Sibley gave up, unwilling to attack the Union entrenchments and superior artillery. He and his men withdrew to their encampments along the river, while the Yanks filed back into their overcrowded fort.

For the next two days, the Rebel troops rested and prepared for the next move while their officers planned and scouts looked for a way to bypass the fort. It was found by George M. Frazer, commander of the Arizona Rangers. Frazer was a thirty-three-year-old veteran of the Mexican-American War who had been a dispatch rider and a wagon master for the

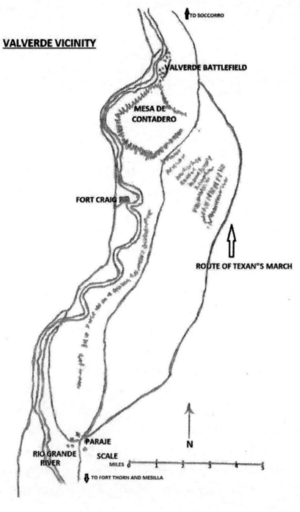

Valverde vicinity.

U.S. Army in the territory, as well as a deputy U.S. marshal, and he also owned an express company. He was as familiar with the country as anyone who was not Apache. He soon found what Sibley needed: a route out of reach of the garrison's artillery that would lead to the Valverde Ford.

His decision made, Sibley sent his men back east to wade across the Rio Grande to campsites at Paraje Fra Cristobal to prepare for their next move. Sibley had decided to commit his little army to a desperate gamble. The army would cut loose from its lines of communication, and only line of retreat south to Mesilla, and swing east around Fort Craig to seize the key river ford at Valverde six miles north of the fort. Sibley correctly believed that this would force Canby to fight for his own line of communication to the north.

The route east of the river led the Confederates across a weathered basaltic mesa some forty to eighty feet above the Rio Grande, with few places of easy access from the river. It rose sharply from the river to a plateau cut by numerous ravines and covered with deep sand drifts in many places. It was difficult but passable for wheeled vehicles, wagons and artillery. The seventeen-mile route would take two days, and men and animals would be without water for the entire trip.

The Rebel move surprised the Yankees. A Union officer wrote later that Confederate movement was "by a road which our engineers declared

Valverde, 1845, from the *Report of Lieutenant James W. Abert*.

impassable." Misunderstanding Sibley's intentions, Canby believed that Sibley was trying to seize the high ground rising east of the river that overlooked the fort. The Federals tried to attack the strung-out Confederate flanks as they moved over the high ground east of the river and in view of the fort. Upon receiving the reports of his scout's detection of the Rebel movement, Canby moved his main force out of the fort. Crossing the frigid Rio Grande, the Federal soldiers occupied the ridges overlooking the fort beyond the east banks of the river to prevent Sibley from emplacing artillery where it could dominate the fort. Actually, the Confederates didn't have artillery with the range and weight needed to reduce the fort anyway. Canby's move forced the Rebels to halt their march and deploy against a threatened flank attack. Colonel Tom Green hurried his forces into position, recognizing that he already held the high ground and hoping to bring on a battle under these favorable conditions. Below them, Canby's men struggled up the sandy ravines to get into position. They had barely reached and formed on the ridgelines when "a few harmless cannon-shots" fired by Captain Trevanion T. Teel's Rebel battery of artillery caused "utter confusion" in Colonel Miguel Pino's regiment of New Mexico Volunteers. They broke and fled in panic, carrying other units with them. The panic-stricken troops could not be rallied on the field, and reluctantly, but not surprised, Canby fell back into the fort, leaving some infantry to prevent the Confederates from emplacing artillery on the heights.

Even before it began the long, cold, waterless march around Fort Craig, the Confederate Army of New Mexico was in bad condition. Men and horses were weakened by disease and starvation. Many men had already died. In the wintry New Mexico desert, the army was "almost destitute of blankets." Except for Scurry's (Baylor's) Second Regiment, who were well armed thanks to their captures from Union troops at San Augustin Pass, the rest were poorly armed: "We were armed with squirrel guns, bear guns, sportsman's guns, shotguns, both single and double barrels, in fact, guns of all sorts." Another remembered that "on leaving home we gathered up all the old shotguns and rifles we could. I had an old shotgun that had two barrels but only one lock, and it was a fair sample, but did effective work; as it sent fifteen buckshot into them at a time." One veteran later claimed that there were only three hundred long-range guns in the entire army. Yet as badly armed as it was, Sibley's army had better munitions than it had food supplies. One veteran remembered that when they were issued three days' rations for the march, they promptly set to "cooking everything they had, trusting alone to God for more." This way they were assured of at least one full meal.

The march proved extremely arduous. The army struggled up sand-choked ravines and then across a sandy, waterless plain cut by numerous ravines. Strong winds whipped up sand and gravel to pummel their skin and thin clothes. It shifted to a north wind driving sleet and snow into the faces of the marching column. The half-starved animals, without water, struggled to pull the wagons and artillery pieces through the deep sand. They had to be helped through the hard places by the soldiers, dragging the guns and wagons through. At night the troops were forced to make a cold, waterless camp on the desert with no food, fuel or blankets. "Another instance of our General's disregard for our welfare and comfort," a soldier diarist complained. During the night (February 20–21), some 150 poorly guarded mules, desperate for water, stampeded toward the river, where they were collected by the Yankees. The loss would soon prove crippling to Sibley's force.

Dawn on February 21, 1862, found the Rebel Army of New Mexico camped along the seventeen-mile route around Fort Craig, cold, hungry and thirsty. The leading element was a portion of Baylor's Second Texas under the command of Major Charles Pyron. Baylor himself had been left in Mesilla as the "civilian" governor of Confederate Arizona because of the mutual dislike between Baylor and Sibley. Pyron had 180 men, including most of Coopwood's San Elizario Company, and at least some of the Brigands.

The Confederate Army of New Mexico's route around Fort Craig led them around a flat-topped volcanic plug called the Mesa del Contadero, which stretched three miles long and one to three miles wide and rose abruptly some three hundred feet from the Rio Grande on its western and northern sides. Beyond the north end of the Mesa, the river made an abrupt western swing from its southerly course to swing around the Mesa. Where the river had turned west it left a wide bed of sand about a mile in length and half a mile in width, stretching from the river's westward bend to the northern edge of the Mesa. It was cut by an ancient abandoned riverbed and covered with scattered cottonwoods that were particularly thick at the northern and the southern ends near the Mesa. Behind the sandy bench, the land rose up steeply to the plateau. To the south the Mesa rose vertically from the end of the level river plain. There were two shallow crossing points, fords, that provided passage to the roads connecting Fort Craig to Albuquerque and its sources of supply and reinforcement. Only the lower one was used by travelers before the battle. The area around the fords was called Valverde for an abandoned village site to the north. It has been known ever since as the location of the bloodiest battle ever fought in the West.

Canby had been surprised by the Confederate march to the ford, but his scouts were closely watching the Rebels and had soon detected the movement. To guard the ford Canby had sent Colonel Jose Valdez and his mounted Third New Mexico Volunteers. Though still uncertain about Confederate intentions, he prepared to reinforce Valdez with a combined arms force of infantry, cavalry and artillery, including some of his most reliable units. By 8:00 a.m. on February 21, 1862, Colonel Benjamin S. Roberts was en route from the fort with a force of infantry (two companies of Regulars, two of volunteers), cavalry (five companies of Regulars

Mesa de Contadera, from Fort Craig, 2011.

and one of volunteers) under Major Thomas Duncan and artillery (two batteries, Captain Alexander McRae's four-gun battery and two twenty-four-pound howitzers under Lieutenant Robert Hall). Battle loomed as the Yankees moved north. "I believe the instruments are well strung and the ball will open soon," one Union soldier confided in his diary.

Actually, the "ball" had already started. Pyron and his 180 men had left their camp at daybreak (about 6:30 a.m.), heading for the river. When he reached the river plain, Pyron at first thought that the ford was unoccupied. His men hurried to the riverbank to water their suffering animals, reaching the thick stand of cottonwoods along the bank above the ford between 7:00 a.m. and 7:30 a.m. They had barely finished filling their canteens and watering their horses when scouts detected Union horsemen downstream on their left, nearer the ford in the cottonwoods.

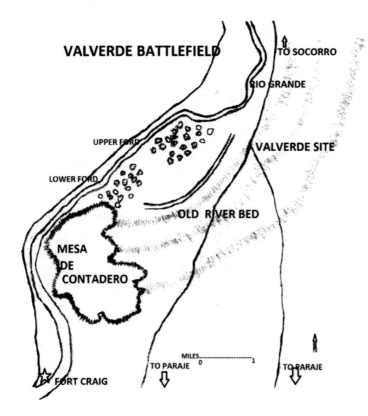

The Valverde battlefield.

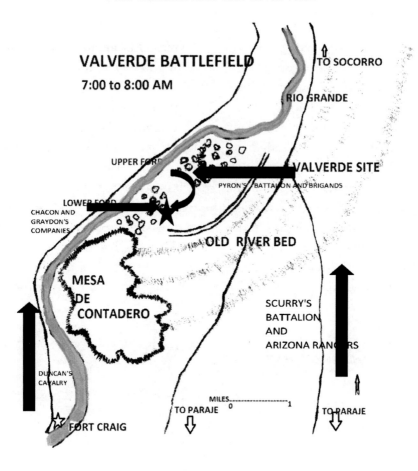

The Valverde battlefield, 7:00 a.m. to 8:00 a.m.

Estimating his foe at four companies, Pyron charged into them, driving the New Mexico Volunteers back into the trees along the river. Here, as his men reached the dry bed of an old river course, Pyron suddenly discovered that he was facing "a large force of all arms." Roberts's men were reaching the ford and crossing to aid the embattled volunteers.

The first of these to arrive were Duncan's cavalrymen, sent ahead of Roberts's main force by Canby, who had become alarmed by the threat to the ford. The leading companies, Graydon's and Rafeal Chacon's, had arrived at the lower ford before 7:00 a.m. It was quickly obvious to the Rebels that "we had bit off more than we could chew," and they sought a defensible position. The Rebel battalion was soon deployed along the bank of the old riverbed, using it for cover. They exchanged fire with the Yankees in the cottonwoods, who were being steadily reinforced. Most of these Rebels were armed with captured long-range rifles and could respond effectively. Pyron's men were aligned near the southern end of the dried-up streambed, close to the Mesa and near the lower ford. The San Elizario Company and the Brigands fought on the north end of the line in the riverbed to offer protection to Pyron's exposed right flank. The unequal fight continued for about an hour before more Confederate troops reached the field.

Facing overwhelming odds that grew worse with each passing minute, Pyron sent a plea to the nearest Confederate unit behind him on the line of march, Colonel William "Dirty Shirt" Scurry's Fourth TMV. The message was carried by Captain John Phillips, the commander of the Brigands who had guided Pyron's men to the river. There were, Pyron reported, "large masses of the enemy" in front of him. Scurry quickly dispatched Major Henry W. Raguet and his battalion, who raced toward the battlefield, led by Phillips. Lieutenant John Reily's light howitzer battery hurried after Raguet's men. Behind them, Scurry pushed the rest of the regiment toward the fords as fast as their horses' condition allowed. Scurry's men were in "high spirits and singing songs" as they rode to the battlefield, a witness recalled. They were led by Captain George Frazer and his Rangers. When they reached the battlefield, Frazer and his Rangers rejoined Pyron's command, where "he did good service" for the remainder of the long, bloody day. Placed on the extreme left of the Confederate position, where the Mesa rose, Frazer and his men successfully thwarted efforts by Union troops to scale the heights and gain a dominant position for their sharpshooters, whose weapons outranged most of the Rebels.

The main struggle centered on the cottonwood bosque (grove) at the base of the Mesa. Like his Union counterpart, Lieutenant Colonel Roberts, Scurry recognized the importance of the position and hurried reinforcements to it as they arrived. He sent a strong force, supported by one of Reily's artillery pieces, into the bosque near the Mesa, hoping to be able to turn Duncan's southern flank.

A Confederate soldier fighting with the Rangers described joining "Captain Frazer's Arizona, Tigers, Lions, Rangers or some other bloodthirsty animals," sniping at the Yankees in the trees. "I thought it was the finest fun in the world for about five minutes," he remembered. Then the Union soldiers started shooting back at him. He took cover behind a large boulder only to have a Union twenty-four-pound howitzer shell score a direct hit on the boulder. It threw up "enough rock to surface about four miles of road." He looked around to suddenly find himself totally alone, "the first and only time that I ever found myself in command of a wing of an army in battle, and immediately ordered a retreat which…was obeyed with alacrity" back to the shelter of the old riverbed, where his commander and the other troops had already fled.

Three times the Confederates attacked, trying to reach the river, and three times they were driven back by Major Thomas Duncan's dismounted cavalrymen. Superior Northern numbers and artillery kept the Rebels from the ford and gradually forced them back. Scurry's men were facing some of the best of the Union forces: the Regular cavalry (five companies), supported by the Third New Mexico and several other companies of New Mexico Cavalry. But it was the Union artillery, firing from the west bank of the Rio Grande, that was decisive. The heavier Union artillery soon silenced Reily's lone gun. The struggle for the bosque seesawed for a time, but the Rebels were eventually driven back to the old riverbed and found themselves pinned down like Pyron's men. While casualties were relatively light because of the protection of the riverbanks, large numbers of horses were killed. Scurry's men were also frustrated by their inability to return fire at the Yankees.

On the west bank of the river, Colonel Benjamin Roberts, a balding Mexican-American War veteran and an important railroad builder in the United States and Russia in prewar years, recognized the opportunity before him. He had carefully reconnoitered the land around the ford some days before, and his trained engineer's eye had recognized the key terrain feature of the battlefield: the bosque at the northern base of the Mesa del Contadero that controlled access to the ford and to the old riverbed, where the Confederates were posted. Hoping to unhinge the left end of the Confederate line and roll it up while he held numerical advantage,

Roberts continually pressed Duncan to move forward and clear the bosque, sending messengers repeatedly across the icy river. A forward movement by Duncan would allow Roberts to cross his artillery to the east bank, where he could enfilade the Confederate position in the old riverbed and dominate the steep, sandy approaches down the bluffs that Confederate reinforcements had to use to reach the field. But Duncan, uncertain of the strength of the Rebels in front of him, and unwilling to test them, refused to move forward and simply ignored Roberts's orders. Finally, Roberts gave up on Duncan and, sending a request to Canby for reinforcements, turned his attention to the Confederate right flank to the north, which was undefended.

Canby was by now convinced that Sibley's objective was the Valverde ford. He began to pull his remaining reliable troops from the east bank of the river opposite Fort Craig and hurry them north to the battle. Two battalions of the Regular infantry under the command of Captain Henry Selden waded the icy river and marched north. They were accompanied by two light artillery pieces to reinforce Captain Alexander McRae's four-gun battery of twelve-pounders. Soon General Canby himself hastened to Valverde, bringing with him Pino's regiment (Second New Mexico Volunteers) and a company of Regular cavalry. Arriving about noon, he assumed command.

About this same time (12:30 p.m.), the bulk (about 670 men, eight companies) of Colonel Tom Green's Fifth TMV regiment reached the battlefield. Green had assumed command from Sibley, who was unable to stay in the saddle any longer. Sibley spent the remainder of the battle in the rear, in an ambulance, drinking. With Green came Captain Trevanion T. Teel with most of the remaining artillery of the army. Lieutenant Colonel John Sutton was soon ordered to follow Green's men with part of his small regiment (Seventh TMV), leaving the wagon trains guarded only by two companies with two light guns.

Roberts soon sent Selden's newly arrived infantry (Wingate and Plympton's Battalions and Dodd's company of Colorado Volunteers) across the river, about half a mile north of Valverde Ford. Wading carefully through the rushing, ice-cold, chest-deep water, they picked their way over the rocky bottom, guns held over their heads. Clambering up the bank, they aligned themselves and pushed forward in obedience to Roberts's order to clear the cottonwood bosque with bayonets. Rafael Chacon's company of New Mexico Volunteers protected their exposed right flank and maintained contact with Duncan's Union cavalrymen near the lower ford. Across the bosque, the infantrymen advanced, at first in line and then from (scattered) tree to tree, all the while keeping up a steady fire on the Confederate line. Scurry quickly saw that Selden's advance would overlap his own line, ordered his men to mount and moved some 250 yards farther north in the streambed. This left a considerable gap in the middle of the Confederate line.

The steadily advancing bluecoats poured a destructive fire on the Confederates, inflicting severe casualties among the horses. With short-range guns, shotguns and pistols mainly, the fighting was left to the few men with "Minié rifles," while the rest could only try to stay under cover. Eventually, the Yankees reached close enough range, and all of the Texans opened up. Selden's troops hesitated and then fell back to the relative safety of the thicker cottonwoods near the river. On their extreme left, where the river curved back to the north, the San Elizario Company had been posted against a bluff on the river. Here they were hidden by trees. As the Union line advanced, Coopwood's company found themselves behind the far left flank of the Federal troopers. When Selden fell back, Coopwood's men captured a number of his soldiers in the trees. But the setback was only temporary, and inexorably the better-armed Unionists pressed Scurry's outnumbered men, threatening to turn the Confederate right flank. On the Confederate left, at the foot of the Mesa, Duncan's men, heavily reinforced, were slowly but steadily making progress toward turning that flank.

At this point (between 2:30 p.m. and 3:00 p.m.) occurred one of the legendary events of the Civil War: the only known charge by lancers. In the early days of the war, before the reality of the new long-ranged rifled muskets was understood, several units on both sides were armed with lances. In the Mexican-American War, units of Mexican lancers had achieved a heroic reputation in combat. Two companies in the Fifth TMV were armed with nine-foot lances and also with revolvers. They were part of the force Scurry was using to try and keep Selden from overrunning his riverbed position. Looking across the battlefield, the Confederates saw a company, at the extreme left (north) of the Union lines, dressed in light gray uniforms. Mistakenly believing that the troops were some unreliable New Mexico Volunteers, Captain Willis L. Lang, commanding one of the lancer companies, beseeched Scurry for permission to attack. Reluctantly, Scurry finally agreed. Although he doubted (correctly) the effectiveness of lances in combat, he saw a chance to turn the Union left flank and slow or stop their advance.

The lancers rode to their deaths, not in brilliant sunlight but rather in snow squalls, for the day had turned cold and bitter. The object of their attack, it turned out, was not New Mexican troops but rather Captain Theodore Dodd's Independent Company of Colorado Volunteers. These were hard men, recruited from the South Park mines, noted for their thieving, drinking, brawling, indiscipline and toughness. Dodd, from Ohio, was a West Point graduate who had taken command of the company after the captain was forced to resign. He and most of the company had been involved in a drunken brawl at Fort Garland. There were seventy-one of Dodd's men waiting for the lancers. About sixty-five Rebel troopers walked, then cantered and finally galloped toward the waiting enemy, who shot them down, almost without any loss to themselves. "Buck and ball," a lead ball and three buckshot fired from a rifled gun, trumped medieval lances. One Coloradan "ran his bayonet through one and then shot the top of his head off." Twenty men fell, and most of the horses were shot. Lang was badly wounded in the groin and, after suffering for nine days, had his slave, who had accompanied him to war, hand him his pistol, and then he ended it. The heroic effort moved witnesses on both sides. It was made, Colonel Roberts wrote, "with audacity and desperation" and was "well worthy of a better cause." The surviving troopers, including the second company of lancers who never received its order to charge, piled their lances up and burned them after the battle. They rearmed themselves with firearms scrounged from the battlefield.

Lang's futile charge may have given the Rebels a little time. The Yankees on the northern end of the battle line, including Dodd's men, drew back toward the northern ford and the artillery—away from the Confederate right flank. But gallant failures do not win battles, and the Rebels soon found themselves in an even more dangerous situation. Selden's men had pushed far enough through the bosque at the foot of the Mesa that Roberts now felt secure in crossing his artillery over the river. There they could better support his plan to flank the Texans' dry riverbed position and drive them from it. Captain Alexander McRae's six-gun battery (two six-pound and four twelve-pound guns) were pulled through the river at the upper crossing. Lieutenant Robert Hall's two-gun battery of twenty-four-pound guns, the heaviest at Fort Craig, soon followed. One twenty-four-pound gun broke an axle in midstream and remained trapped there until after the battle, when it was recovered—treacherously under a flag of truce, the Rebels claimed. To support them, Roberts assigned two companies of Regular infantry (Brotherton's and Ingraham's) and two companies of volunteers (Hubbell's and Mortimer's). The Confederates attempted to counter with their own lighter and fewer guns but were quickly silenced as they had been earlier. The guns were then withdrawn to the extreme right flank in reserve to counter the expected Union onslaught at that point.

When Canby arrived on the battlefield and took command, he adopted Roberts's plan to turn the left flank of the Confederate position near the Mesa. Northern firepower had already driven the Rebels away from the lower ford and the Mesa and silenced their artillery, and the Union guns were close to reaching an enfilade position from which Lieutenant Hall's remaining twenty-four-pound gun would make the riverbed position untenable. At the other end of the Confederate line, Scurry's men were also being threatened by the combined fire of the Federal infantry and McRae's battery. After a midafternoon lull during which both armies ate (if they had anything to eat) and refilled their ammunition pouches, the Union forces renewed their assault with increased vigor. With the arrival of the last of Green's regiment and Sutton's battalion, the Confederates had every available soldier on the field, yet they were steadily losing ground, especially on the Confederate left, where Major Samuel Lockridge struggled to keep his men on line under the heaviest fire of the day. Despite their tenacious heroism, they were gradually forced back up (north) the riverbed and closer to the time when the Union artillery could move forward and fire directly along their position.

Both Canby and Green recognized that the decisive moment had come. The Union general, in what proved to be a fatal decision, moved McRae's battery several hundred yards northeast, where it was closer to the Rebel lines but was more exposed. On the other side, Green began massing his troops on the right center of his line, where they were out of sight in the dry riverbed. The movement was not seen. Green had decided on an audacious gamble: to fling most of his troops into a direct assault on the Union artillery. In reality, Green had few options, and none of them was good. Superior Union firepower was inexorably driving in his left flank and was close to achieving a position from which it could dominate the Confederate lines. The Confederates were no longer able to stop them. The Rebel soldiers were hungry, thirsty and fatigued after a day's fighting and were low on ammunition. It was even doubtful that an orderly retreat was possible. Union guns could cover the few passable routes up the steep, sandy hills to the rear. Much of the Rebel force now lacked horses, and the route back to Paraje, for an army that hadn't had water for nearly two days, was probably too long for the men and horses to survive. It seemed that the day was won for the Union. A.A. Mills, serving as an officer on Canby's staff, observed that the Confederates must starve, fight or surrender. Colonel Tom Green chose to fight.

The immediate threat was on the Confederate left, and here Green ordered Raguet's battalion of the Fourth TMV (about 200 to 240 men) to charge (on horseback) Hall's twenty-four-pounder gun that was wreaking havoc. Sometime after 3:00 p.m., Raguet's men left the shelter of the riverbed and charged across the open ground toward the enemy six hundred yards away. Their route took them diagonally across the front of Duncan's force, which had been reinforced by Colonel Kit Carson's First New Mexico Volunteer Regiment, the most reliable of the volunteers, and Captain Paddy Graydon's spy company. At two hundred yards, the Northerners opened fire, decimating Raguet's command, particularly the horses. A twenty-four-pound shell landing in their midst completed the carnage. Recognizing that he could never carry the Union position, Raguet hastily turned his men toward the shelter of the old riverbed. There he tried to reestablish a line of defense with the few men and one small gun that he could rally. Some of his men had simply continued to retreat into the hills. Outnumbered five to one, he hoped to be able to hold out long enough.

Raguet's attack proved to have serious consequences for the Union cause. Duncan and Carson quickly pressed their advantage, pursuing the retreating Rebels and pressing nearer to the decisive southern flank. This took them southeast, farther away from the Union center. The ever cautious Duncan, convinced that he was being attacked by stronger forces than he was, sent to Canby for reinforcements that he didn't need. Alarmed by the volume of gunfire, Canby dispatched Ingraham's company of Plympton's battalion, which was in support of McRae's battery, and then ordered Wingate's battalion to move to the right to support Duncan also. The result was an eight-hundred-yard gap in the Union line and a weakened support for McRae's battery. There should have been enough troops left around the battery for its security, but most of them were New Mexico Volunteers. One Colorado Volunteer noted there were "250 white men and 1,000 greasers" on one side of the guns and "500 white men and 2,000 greasers" on the other. While his numbers were wrong, there should have been enough to protect the guns.

The storming force that Green secretly amassed consisted of about 750 men, including most of his own Fifth TMV regiment and part of Scurry's Fourth, as well as Pyron's battalion and part of Sutton's battalion. In support were the surviving guns of Teel and Reily's batteries. With Pyron's men, the San Elizario Company, Arizona Rangers and Brigands all charged, acting as frontline infantry. The Rebels came in three waves twenty yards apart. They had to charge across six hundred yards of an open sandy plain into the fire of an almost equal number of enemy riflemen and McRae's six-gun battery. Their own weapons were too short ranged to be effective until they were within thirty to fifty yards of the Union lines. On they came, trotting or walking, their officers in the front ranks (ostensibly part of the assaulting force) not really commanding it but rather leading it in the Southern tradition. These Rebels were supremely confident, in themselves and one another. The only command they got was, "Come on boys!—and away they go, every man for himself." Union artillery hammered at them, and it seemed as though hundreds were being slaughtered. Actually, the advancing Confederate soldiers had already learned to watch for the flash of enemy guns when they fired and then to fling themselves to the ground, allowing the shells to pass harmlessly overhead. Their casualties were heavy: 230 killed and wounded, almost 10 percent for the entire battle but comparatively light for a direct assault into the prepared artillery over open ground.

The Rebel assault was launched between 3:30 p.m. and 4:00 p.m. One of the first Union officers to spot the Confederate movement was General Canby himself. He sat astride "Old Chas," his favorite horse, wearing the same old blue woolen shirt that he always wore and chewing a cold cigar, always in his mouth but never lit. Realizing that Plympton's battalion of Regulars was unaware of the Confederate advance and under the shelter of the riverbank behind the artillery, Canby hurried to bring them into action. Before he could finish, the New Mexico Volunteers supporting the artillery broke and ran even before the Confederates reached the range at which their weapons could be effective. Fleeing first to the riverbank and then across it, the volunteers carried with them many of Plympton's Regulars, leaving the rest disorganized and demoralized. Canby hastened to bring up his immediate reserve force, Colonel Miguel Pino's Second New Mexico Cavalry. Despite their officer's efforts, most of the regiment refused to cross the river except for the one company already across. Canby, now on foot ("Old Chas" had been killed), tried to organize support from Wingate's men to the south and from Selden to the north, but both were too far away to render timely support to McRae's now fatally exposed battery.

Around the guns, bitter hand-to-hand fighting decided the ownership of the all-important artillery. At close range, the Confederates found that their shotguns gave them a distinct advantage. "Never were double-barreled shot-guns and rifles used to better effect," Colonel Green observed. Nearly half of the men of McRae's battery fell on the field, including McRae himself, and casualties were heavy among the Regular infantry who fought to save the guns. But the headlong rush of the Confederates could not be denied. Sutton and Lockridge both fell just as they led their men to success. One of the first two Rebels to reach the guns was a private from the San Elizario Company. The Confederates quickly turned the captured guns on the fleeing Yankees wading the river, and Teel's light guns moved up and soon joined in the fight on the riverbank. Hastening back from the right, the U.S. Regular Cavalry under Captain Richard Lord and Wingate's infantry attempted a counterattack to regain the guns. It fell apart when Wingate was wounded and the Confederates were reinforced. Reluctantly, Canby now ordered a general retreat of all of his forces back to Fort Craig. This included Duncan's and Carson's victorious men, who were pursuing Raguet's scattered troops. The exuberant Southerners chased the retreating Northerners across the river, slaughtering many in the river itself. But when they attempted to cross the river and pursue Canby's men to Fort Craig, Green stopped them. An hour later, when a flag of truce was forwarded by Canby, Green agreed to a two-day truce to tend the wounded and the dead.

Green's decision to accept a truce was controversial at the time and remains so to this day. He had good reasons. His men were scattered, tired, hungry and low on ammunition, and it was already dark. Canby's force, though defeated, was still strong. Green also may have thought that the truce was a prelude to Canby's surrender of the fort. But Canby had no intention of surrendering the post. He could count rations as well as anyone and knew that he still held the high cards. However, most of the Rebel Army of New Mexico came, in time, to feel that a golden opportunity was lost by agreeing to the truce. For his part, Canby and his troops blamed the failure of the New Mexico troops for their defeat, although some U.S. Regulars (two companies) had also broken and some New Mexico Volunteers (Kit Carson's First New Mexico Volunteer Regiment) had fought courageously and effectively. Most interestingly, the backbone of Canby's force had been his U.S. Regulars, well trained and equipped and led by West Point trained officers who were soundly beaten by Texas farm boys armed with shotguns and led by amateurs. One of the Rebels noted that "Colonel Green knows nothing about military science but he knows how to fight and win battles." Both sides suffered heavy casualties: 17 percent for the Union and 10 percent for the Rebels. The loss of Rebel field officers was especially heavy. The condition of the wounded, scattered throughout the dark battlefield, was pitiable. As night fell, search parties from both armies scoured the battlefield with improvised torches looking for the wounded before they froze. The burial parties treated their enemies with "chivalry and courtesy" when they met on the dark field.

The capture of McRae's battery and the victory at Valverde quickly attained mythic status in the Texas Confederacy. The guns themselves became objects of veneration. Many men must have felt like A.B. Peticolas when he said: "I thought that I had experienced a good many moments of exquisite pleasure, but never before have I felt such perfect happiness as I did when we took the battery from our enemy." It would remain as the high point of the campaign and the proudest achievement of the Confederate Army of New Mexico. The Rebels had won a heroic and almost miraculous victory, but there proved to be few fruits to gather.

In fact, the situation of the army was now truly desperate. The day after the battle, Sibley gathered his senior officers for a council of war to consider their options. The army had only three days' rations left. It lacked the strength to capture Fort Craig and its supplies. The army could return to the Mesilla–El Paso area, but the army had already exhausted the food supplies there. The only place it could get supplies was from the Union depots to the north, especially Fort Union. But the army was also burdened with a large number of sick and wounded who had to be cared for and for whom there was no shelter. Also, the army was now partially dismounted. Hundreds of horses and mules had been killed, died of disease or had been lost. This meant that if they went north, their progress would be slow, and they would have to leave at Fort Craig a powerful enemy across their lines of supply or retreat. Even if they went north, there was no guarantee that they would be able to capture the supplies they needed. But there really was no other alternative, and the army soon began preparing to march north. The dead were buried in a large mass grave, and the wounded, who were dying at an alarming rate, were prepared for movement. Prisoners were paroled. Excess baggage and wagons were burned. By midday on February 23, the Confederate Army of New Mexico slowly and painfully began its fateful journey north along the sandy road that followed the Rio Grande.

Chapter 5

Albuquerque and Santa Fe

G eneral Canby had been quicker to understand the reality of the Rebels' condition than the Rebels. Immediately after the Battle of Valverde, he had sent Major James L. Donaldson, his chief quartermaster officer, out of Fort Craig by a circuitous mountain route. Donaldson had authority to act in Canby's name and to remove or destroy everything that the Rebels might use and then to gather the scattered Union troops in the north into Fort Union. Canby already knew that Union reinforcements were coming from Colorado. Canby also moved to "disembarrass" himself of the unreliable New Mexico troops by simply sending the militia home and sending the unreliable volunteers away from the war zone. Many had already deserted in the aftermath of Valverde, including an entire company along with its captain. Canby retained the most reliable units, like Carson's regiment at Fort Craig and Graydon's scout company.

Accompanying Major Donaldson were the remnants (280 men) of the Second New Mexico militia regiment that had not already deserted. Commanded by Colonel Nicholas Pino and Major Charles F. Wesche, the unit had already reached Polvadera when it was ordered to return south to defend Socorro from a Confederate raiding force. The Rebel force consisted of five mounted companies of the Fifth TMV under young Lieutenant Colonel Henry McNeill. A year before, McNeill, a Mississippi-born West Pointer, had been a lieutenant in the (U.S.) First

Dragoons stationed at Fort Stanton. With McNeill were George Frazer's Arizona Rangers and some of the San Elizario Company and Brigands. McNeill was surprised to find Union forces in the little adobe town when he approached on the evening of February 24. He quickly deployed his men on high ground southwest of town and sent the irregulars under Frazer to seal off the road north. When McNeill's light artillery piece fired one round over the town, most of Pino's regiment promptly disappeared into the darkness. After vainly playing for time, hoping for reinforcements, Pino was forced to surrender his remaining 37 men in the early morning hours. That morning, 150 more men of the regiment reappeared from hiding, eager to surrender and affix their names to paroles and thereby avoid further service.

The captures at Socorro gave the Army of New Mexico new logistical life. Some eight hundred barrels of flour and other food, three hundred guns, medical supplies, three hundred horses and mules and many wagons were taken. At Stapleton's ranch store, near Valverde, considerable food and clothing had been captured. Stapleton was serving as a militia officer. North of Socorro, a small wagon train carrying food to Fort Craig was later taken at Las Lunas on March 1. Together, these acquisitions gave the army enough, barely, to reach Albuquerque. A hospital was established at Socorro, giving the sick and wounded their first shelter in weeks. They would be left there when the army moved on to the north, safe in the knowledge that the chivalrous Yankees would not molest them. Camped north of town, the army now prepared for the march to Fort Union.

The main preparation was to dismount the Fourth TMV. So many horses and mules had been lost that the army was in serious straits. The losses at Valverde had been particularly heavy in the Fourth, but all of the regiments had shortages of animals. Each regiment was partially mounted and partially afoot. This was an impossible situation either on the march or in battle. It was complicated further by the fact that most of Sibley's men owned their own horses and equipment. After lengthy discussions among the senior officers it was decided to dismount one regiment, the Fourth TMV, and distribute their remaining horses among the other regiments. It was a bitter pill to swallow for Texans anytime but particularly so to be left on foot in the midst of their enemies in an alien desert. An impassioned appeal to the patriotism of the men of the Fourth by its commander, Colonel William Scurry, carried the day, and the Fourth surrendered their horses and became "footpads." The men of the Fourth were promised that they would be paid for their horses and equipment, typically about $100 to $150 (a private soldier made $11 per month). But they never were paid.

Ahead of them, their heroic sacrifices were being undone by vigorous Yankee actions. Upon reaching Albuquerque, Major Donaldson informed his assistant quartermaster, Captain Herbert Enos, of the disaster at Valverde and ordered him to ensure that none of the supplies at the large Albuquerque depot fell into Southern hands. Donaldson then hurried on to Santa Fe to oversee the evacuation of the territorial government and Fort Marcy, as well as all of the supplies, to Fort Union. Enos only had twelve men at the Albuquerque depot, but he prepared to do his best. He knew that he couldn't move the large volume of supplies, and so he planned to destroy them. But he also knew that the local population was eagerly waiting and watching for the depot to be abandoned so that they, desperately poor in 1862, could loot it. The depot therefore had to be destroyed quickly and upon short notice. Enos decided to burn the supplies by setting fire to the buildings. He waited until he had unequivocal word that the Rebels were near. This came on the evening of March 1, when Enos learned that Rebels had reached Belen, thirty miles south.

Early the next morning, the depot was set afire, and Enos and his men headed north, taking only the ammunition stores with them. As he feared, the townspeople rushed in to save what they could from the burning buildings but most of the food was lost. The Rebels, marching from the south, could see before them all day the column of smoke that marked the end of their dream. Upon reaching Albuquerque, the Rebels found "a pool of grease, three or four feet deep, just in front of their commissary building," where the army's bacon had been stored. Actually, some supplies escaped destruction, and more were recovered from the civilians in town. Local store owners reluctantly provided more food and clothing in return for Confederate IOUs. The Armijo brothers (Manuel and Rafael) were rich merchants and the sons of the last Mexican governor. They turned over some $200,000 (an immense sum in 1862) worth of goods in their stores and warehouses to Sibley's quartermaster and joined the Confederate cause themselves. One of the last acts of the Confederate Congress in April 1865 was an appropriation to recompense the Armijo brothers for their losses. Altogether, the Rebels got enough supplies to carry them in the short term, but not for very long.

One of the many mysteries of the New Mexico campaign was why Sibley failed to send his excellent cavalry on a deep lightning-like thrust to seize the supplies he needed at either Albuquerque or Fort Union before they could be destroyed. It was not until February 28 when Major Charles Pyron was sent ahead of the main force with his battalion of the Second TMV (Baylor's old command) and the irregular scout or "spy" companies raised in New Mexico. By then it was far too late. The Northerners had had enough time to move or destroy the needed supplies.

Then, out of nowhere, luck came to the Rebel army in the unlikely form of an alcoholic physician commanding a three-man army of gamblers. Cubero was a small army post located about thirty-five miles west of Albuquerque. It served primarily as a supply depot for campaigns against the Navajos, whose homeland was still farther west. A considerable quantity of stores were there in March 1862, apparently forgotten by the

Cubero. *Courtesy of the Museum of New Mexico.*

Northern command. There was also a small garrison of forty-five New Mexico troops commanded by Captain Francisco Aragon. The troops already knew of the appearance of Sibley's army at Socorro when Dr. Finis E. Kavanaugh suddenly appeared at the remote post.

Kavanaugh was a Santa Fe physician, famous for his stable of fast horses, his hard drinking and his gambling. Already dying from alcoholism and/or tuberculosis, the lanky and cadaverous doctor and his brother were wealthy merchants who mingled in the upper levels of territorial society, such as they were. Kavanaugh was particularly noted for courting all of the available young women, although he was much older. Actually, Kavanaugh was also secretly maintaining a family with a New Mexican wife and five children on his ranch. Pro-Southern in outlook, the Missouri-born doctor attempted to stay out of the conflict, but the constant humiliation and harassment by Union officials finally led him to decide to join the South.

Recruiting three of his gambling buddies of Southern inclination, he rode to Cubero, where Kavanaugh held the contract as post trader and had a large store. There, at 9:00 a.m. on March 3, they demanded of the astonished Captain Aragon that he surrender immediately or else the "Kavanaugh Regiment" was prepared to attack. Aragon quickly surrendered, and one of the regiment, Richmond Gillespie, undertook the hazardous journey to the Rebel army, alone through Navajo country, to bring men to secure the logistical bonanza. Captain Alfred Thurman and Company A of the Seventh TMV soon arrived at the obscure little post to secure the logistical treasure. Some twenty-five wagonloads were soon en route to Albuquerque, and much more was sent later as transport became available. The supplies, added to what had already been taken, were sufficient to carry the small army for several weeks. Kavanaugh later returned to Texas with Sibley's army and served as both a Confederate field officer (a cavalry major) and as a medical officer. At war's end, he refused to surrender and died in Mexico in 1866.

The Army of New Mexico no longer faced imminent starvation, but its strategic situation had grown worse. Strong reinforcements were coming to Fort Union from Colorado, and the Confederates would be located between two strong Union forces who lurked in forts, impregnable to the

Rebels, ready to strike at them when the moment was right. The army still lacked transport for wagons and artillery. The shortage of horses and mules grew worse each day as more died. Ammunition was also becoming a problem. Here, too, Sibley had thought that he could capture enough to resupply his forces. Perhaps worst of all, there did not seem to be a decisive target that the army might strike to achieve a decision.

The Army of New Mexico trickled into Albuquerque on the seventh and eighth of March, ending a long, cold, hard march on inadequate rations. The countryside had suffered when they marched through, as the Rebel troops seized whatever they needed from the natives. While it was necessary to impress food and fodder and firewood, there was also widespread looting. Like soldiers everywhere given license to seize property, they proved uncontrollable, stealing freely and destroying much more. The native New Mexicans, who were extremely poor, had already suffered heavily at the hands of the undisciplined New Mexico militia and volunteers, who had exacted a heavy toll, impressing property and looting. Record floods in the early summer of 1862, coming after an extremely bitter winter, meant that the territory soon faced mass starvation.

The indiscriminate looting had worsened an already intense hatred of Texans by Spanish-speaking New Mexicans. The historic enmity had its roots in the atrocities committed by Mexican troops during Texas's struggle for independence and the later Texans' retaliations. Much of Sibley's strategy had been based on his assumption, gathered when he was stationed in prewar New Mexico, that the natives were so disaffected from the federal government that they would flock to his colors. One of his first acts upon arriving in the territory was to issue a proclamation in December 1861 assuring the native New Mexicans of good treatment by the Confederacy and urging them to join his cause. Much to the chagrin of Union authorities, Sibley managed to distribute his proclamations widely throughout New Mexico by clandestine means. From Albuquerque he issued yet another. The reaction was the same as the first: nothing. Save for a few "ricos," almost no Hispanic New Mexicans ever joined the Confederates. Another of the pillars of Sibley's strategy proved spectacularly hollow.

Sibley knew that his little army needed time to recuperate, but it was time he didn't really have. Union reinforcements were being rushed to Fort Union from Colorado. Nevertheless, the army paused around Albuquerque for nearly two weeks. There was now plenty of food, but little firewood or fodder for the horses and mules. Sibley decided to send the bulk of his force into the Sandia Mountains east of Albuquerque, where there was grass and firewood. Several companies of the Fifth TMV were retained in the city as guards. Pyron's battalion of the Second TMV (Baylor's regiment) and the irregular units were sent on toward

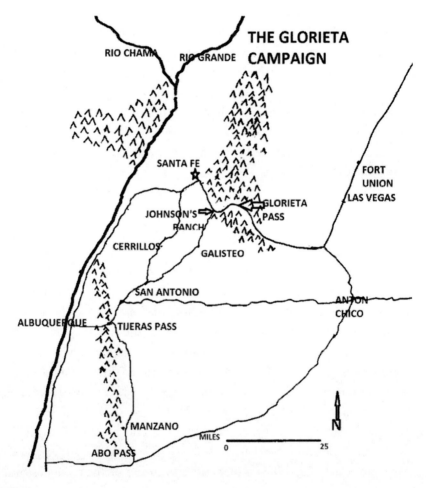

The Glorieta campaign.

Santa Fe to watch developments. A single company of the Seventh was kept at Cubero to guard supplies there.

Sending the men into the Sandias proved to be a mistake. The cold and snow, always accompanied by strong winds in New Mexico, soon wreaked havoc on the health of the troops. Their inadequate clothing, lack of blankets and tents that had been abandoned made them vulnerable to pneumonia and other respiratory diseases. The men crowded into a few huts and caves. Sickness swept through the camps. Sibley's army would lose nearly one-third of its men to disease on this campaign, many times more than those lost to Yankee bullets.

The Brigands and other scouts continued to probe toward Santa Fe. There the energetic Major Donaldson was efficiently carrying out his orders to leave nothing for the Rebels. Deciding that Santa Fe was militarily indefensible, Donaldson oversaw the movement of the territorial government, including Governor Henry Connelley, to Fort Union. Sibley gave him enough time. Some 120 wagonloads of supplies were evacuated and the rest set afire, but some was later recovered by the Southerners. On March 4, the remaining Federal soldiers marched out of the city toward Fort Union. Donaldson reported that on the night march an entire battalion of New Mexico troops deserted except for a few officers, including Lieutenant Colonel Manuel Chavez.

Confederate scouts hovered around Santa Fe and the roads east, watching the Union withdrawal, but Sibley made no move to interfere. They also scoured the countryside for supplies and sometimes met and tangled with Union cavalry patrols. Bill Davidson proudly boasted in later years that he and some comrades "had performed the greatest feat of the war," for which he deserved a commission. They, just 4 men, had made a company (120 men) of "Yanks," Regular cavalry, ride faster than they ever had in their lives. Unfortunately for Davidson, they were chasing him at the time. Somehow he outran them on a newly captured U.S. Army mule to reach Major John Shropshire's command. "Oh! How glad I was to see him," he recalled.

Five days after the Federal evacuation of Santa Fe, the first Rebel scouts rode in. These were eleven Brigands led by Captain John Phillips, who promptly took his notorious band to his former gambling emporium,

The southeastern corner of the Santa Fe Plaza and the Exchange Hotel, 1858. *Courtesy of the Museum of New Mexico.*

the Exchange Hotel, for a drunken celebration. The next day, Major Alexander Jackson, the prewar territorial secretary, arrived with seventy more of the western irregulars. On March 13, Pyron arrived with the rest of his battalion. The Rebels quickly spread throughout the city, seeking whatever supplies could still be had. They found that a number of soldiers' families had remained in the city, including Mrs. Louisa Canby, the wife of the Union commanding general. The families were treated with great courtesy and respect by the Rebels, in contrast to the treatment already being accorded to civilians in the South.

Chapter 6

Glorieta

On March 21, 1862, the alcohol-soaked commander of the Confederate Army of New Mexico finally put his tattered legions into motion. Sibley had known since December 1861 that troops from Colorado were on their way to reinforce the Fort Union garrison. He could not have expected them to arrive as quickly as they did, arriving on the same day, March 11, that Pyron reached Santa Fe with his small battalion. Sibley, however, was showing few signs of any sense of urgency to reach Fort Union. He had plenty of reasons or excuses: the severe winter weather, the condition of his horses and men, the need to rest and refit and the scarcity of horses and mules—all inhibited the Confederate advance.

In reality, the only hope the Confederates had of victory in New Mexico was the quick seizure of Fort Union and its immense stores. However, the impetus of the (so far) successful invasion withered away around the pathetic little fires that the soldiers built to warm themselves as they waited in the cold and windy mountains east of Albuquerque. Sibley was finally stirred into action by intelligence that the Colorado troops had arrived at Fort Union and that Canby was preparing to sorty from Fort Craig. With his army in between the two Union forces, Sibley could not afford to allow them to meet and combine forces. He chose to move first against the weaker of the two: the Fort Union garrison.

Sibley, who had once commanded Fort Union and understood the terrain, expected the Federal forces to defend Fort Union in the easily defensible canyons at Glorieta Pass, some seventy-five miles south of the fort. To circumvent this, Sibley planned to send three separate columns toward the pass. If the Union forces made a stand anywhere along the pass, they would theoretically be outflanked by one or the other of the Confederate columns swinging to the east and south of the mountains. To reinforce Pyron, he sent his best mounted troops, Major John Shropshire's battalion of the Fifth TMV (Companies A, B, C and D), about two hundred men, to Santa Fe. Pyron was expected to move through the pass from west (Santa Fe) to east along the Santa Fe Trail. Colonel John Scurry commanded the largest of the Rebel wings, nearly eight hundred men of the Fourth TMV (minus Company A) and four companies of the Seventh TMV under Major Powhatan Jordan, a physician turned soldier. These forces were to move northeast through Galisteo, follow Galisteo Creek and join Pyron at the west entrance to Glorieta Pass. Colonel Tom Green, with six companies of the Fifth TMV, remained east of Albuquerque, where they could watch for Canby's approach from the south or swing east to Anton Chico and outflank any Union force defending Glorieta Pass against Scurry and Pyron's advance. Another company remained at Cubero guarding supplies, and two companies were left to hold Albuquerque.

Ahead of them, new enemies waited for the Rebels. The Union reinforcements had been long in coming from Colorado. William Gilpin, who had been appointed territorial governor in 1861 by Lincoln, was a West Point graduate, a Mexican-American War veteran and one of the most experienced explorers in the West. But he was also a visionary who sometimes did not have a firm grip on reality. As the war had spread in 1861, Gilpin became convinced that Confederates and/or Indians were about to overrun the territory. In the imaginary crisis, he took vigorous action, raising a fourteen-company, 2,700-man military force; building Camp Weld in Denver at the exorbitant cost of $40,000; arresting hundreds of suspected Southern sympathizers and holding them without trial; and imposing martial law. He did all of this at a cost of $355,000 (an extraordinary amount in 1861), without any legal authorization, by simply issuing vouchers on the government. Even his soldiers were paid in IOUs. When Washington learned with horror of Gilpin's imaginative financing, the debts were repudiated, although most were eventually paid, and Gilpin was fired.

What Gilpin did not do was use his army. It stayed near Denver, and Gilpin refused to send the help that General Canby needed and requested. After Gilpin traveled to Washington to answer his critics in December 1861, the territory was temporarily left in the hands of Lewis Weld, the territorial secretary and a much more realistic man. When Canby again appealed for help, Weld, on his own authority, sent Captain Theodore Dodd's Independent Company (Infantry), which arrived at Fort Craig just in time for the Battle of Valverde. Later, Captain James H. Ford led his Independent Company of Cavalry south through the cold and deep snow to Santa Fe. They arrived on March 4, just in time to join Major Donaldson and the retreat to Fort Union. But two companies were not enough to ensure the safety of New Mexico, and again Canby appealed for aid, on February 12. This time Weld ordered the ten companies of the First Colorado Volunteer Infantry Regiment to Fort Union as fast as they could travel.

The companies of the First Colorado Volunteer Infantry Regiment had been recruited in the mining camps in the mountains and in Denver, where there were large numbers of destitute men, stranded by the exhaustion of the mines. These were tough, hardy, adventurous, lawless and undisciplined men. For months the volunteers kept Denver in a tumult with their drunken brawls, nightly thieving forays, murder and even mutiny. When Canby's call came, the people of Denver were vastly relieved to see the volunteers depart. From Denver Colonel John Slough led seven companies, while three more left Fort Lyon to join en route under Lieutenant Colonel Samuel Tappan. Slough was an Ohio-born lawyer whose wealthy family contributed large sums to equip the regiment, while Tappan was a New York newspaperman from an extreme Abolitionist family. Neither had any appreciable military experience, but each possessed abundant personal ambition and political zeal. There were doubts that the regiment could reach Fort Union in time.

They left Denver on February 22, the day after Valverde, although they didn't learn of the battle for several days. There was then no appreciable force between Sibley's Rebels and the undermanned fort, and they were much closer. But when Sibley delayed, the Coloradans got ahead of him. The First Regiment of Colorado Volunteer Infantry performed one of history's greatest wartime marches. The 950 volunteers covered four hundred miles in thirteen days in severe winter weather, the last ninety-two miles in an incredible thirty-six hours, facing a winter gale. They had been falsely alarmed by reports that one thousand Rebels were closing in on Fort Union. They arrived on the same day, March 11, that Pyron reached Santa Fe with his small battalion totaling eighty-one men.

The commander of Fort Union was a forty-nine-year-old Mexican-American War veteran, Colonel Gabriel Paul, who now saw a chance for the military glory that had so far eluded him in his lengthy army career.

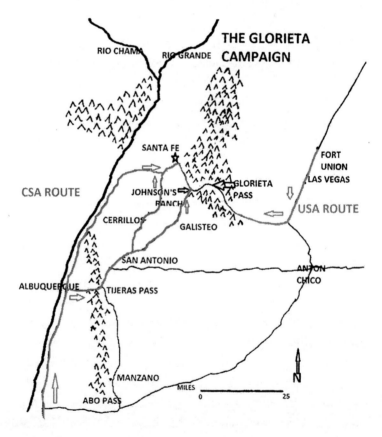

The Battle of Glorieta Pass.

To his horror, he found that Slough, the newly appointed commanding officer of the First Colorado Volunteers, outranked him by virtue of a few days' seniority. Furthermore, Slough, who had only a few weeks' military experience, planned to take command of the field force being organized by Paul to move against the Rebels. Deprived of his chance for military fame, Paul suddenly found all sorts of reasons why Slough should not take the offensive, although he had planned to do the same thing himself. Chief of these were the orders of General Canby, still in Fort Craig, that strictly enjoined Paul, who he thought was still in command, not to do anything that might hazard Fort Union and to wait for him to join up before taking any serious offensive action. Canby did authorize Paul, and later Slough, to undertake small-scale harassment of the Rebels and to conduct reconnaissance. He also allowed the Fort Union commander freedom of action in case of unexpected circumstances.

It wasn't much, but it was enough of a loophole for the lawyer turned soldier, Colonel John Slough, and he marched off to Santa Fe 105 miles away with almost the entire Fort Union garrison and artillery on March 22, 1862. Behind him, Slough left a fuming and frustrated Colonel Paul, who promptly gathered up the correspondence between himself, Slough and Canby. He forwarded it to the adjutant general of the United States Army, petulantly writing, "My object in this communication is to throw the responsibility of any disaster which may occur on the right shoulders." Paul got his chance for glory at Gettysburg, where he was blinded by a Confederate bullet.

Preceded by the Brigands acting as scouts, Pyron's small force, including Shropshire's battalion, left Santa Fe on March 25, 1862. Pyron had with him about 280 men, including Shropshire's, the Brigands and some other irregulars. The tall, handsome Shropshire, beloved by his troops, had no illusions about the predicament of the army. He wrote his wife that "a fight there [in the open field] was our only salvation," for the Confederates lacked the resources to take Fort Union. "Some of us will have an opportunity to make an end to our glorious careers," he predicted uncannily for himself. Surprisingly, the Confederate maneuvers, as at Valverde, did succeed in drawing the Union forces into the open field for battle, but like at Valverde, the result was not what the Rebels hoped for.

The Brigands led Pyron's men down the Santa Fe Trail to the southeast and east. For a few miles, the trail climbed over a low divide and then crossed a shelving plateau, dropping from the Sangre de Christo Mountains to the north and cut by a number of (dry) arroyos, large and small. About 15.0 miles from Santa Fe, the trail entered a narrow defile, Apache Canyon, which separates the Sangre de Christo Mountains to the north from the Glorieta Mesa to the south. Galisteo Creek, usually dry, enters the canyon at this point from the southwest, flowing through its own canyon. Near this point, in 1862, stood Johnson's Ranch, a stagecoach way station on the Santa Fe Trail. From here the trail climbed the narrow canyon, less than one hundred yards wide in many places but becoming wider as it climbed to the northeast, 4.1 miles to Glorieta Pass, gaining about one thousand feet in elevation. The trail turned east and then southeast through a widening valley, 2.2 miles to Pigeon's Ranch, about two hundred feet lower than the pass. Today the pass is nearly filled in its narrow places by a railroad and Interstate 25. The ranch was owned by a French immigrant, Alexander Valle, known as "Pigeon" for his distinctive dancing style. It was an important station on the Santa Fe Trail and was composed of numerous buildings, corrals and sheds.

Pyron's men reached Johnson's Ranch after dark on March 25 and made scattered camps in the vicinity. The night soon turned bitterly cold, and the Rebels, lacking enough warm clothes or blankets, spent most of the night huddled around their campfires in vain efforts to keep warm. Few got much sleep. Their officers allowed them to remain in camp the next morning until the sun warmed the air enough that they could get some sleep. Thus, at midday on March 26, most of Pyron's men were scattered about Johnson's Ranch napping in the warm sun, guarded by the Brigands on lookout east of Pigeon's Ranch. Unknown to the sleeping men, a column of 418 bluecoats had already entered the other end of the long pass, heading toward them.

Slough commanded 1,342 men, of which most (916 men) were from his own regiment, the First Colorado Volunteers. He also had four companies of Regular cavalry from the First and Third U.S. Cavalry and eight guns in two batteries. They reached Bernal Springs, forty-five miles south of Fort Union, on March 25, and they camped. At this point, where the Santa Fe Trail turned west through the mountains, Slough could watch for the Confederates coming from Albuquerque or Santa Fe while also being able to bottle up the Rebels in a narrow place if they advanced. The Federal officers were unaware that the Santa Fe Rebels had been reinforced by Shropshire's battalion, so Slough sent Major John Chivington and 418 men on toward Glorieta. They planned to surprise Pyron's small force (81 men) in Santa Fe and, hopefully, seize the town. Chivington's men left Bernal Springs about 3:00 p.m. and reached Kozlowski's Ranch, near the ancient Pecos Mission, about midnight.

Chivington was a big (six-foot-four, 280 pounds), loudmouthed, Ohio-born Methodist minister with a reputation as a bully. He was the leading Methodist clergyman in Colorado. When the Colorado Volunteers were organized, Chivington joined but had refused to serve as a chaplain and had instead demanded a combat command, which he got. Chivington had been known to put loaded pistols on his pulpit as he preached in the rough mining towns when local toughs threatened his missionary efforts. He was as loved by his rough troops as the distant and urbane Slough was hated. Slough, somewhat deservedly, feared assassination by his own men to such an extent that he had to create within the regiment a secret thirty-man body of informers and bodyguards from his home region of Ohio. Chivington had a strain of viciousness in him, which showed in his orders to take no prisoners in 1863, the murder of five Confederate guerrillas in 1864 and the infamous Sand Creek Massacre in which as many as five hundred peaceful Cheyenne Indians were slaughtered upon his command. At Glorieta, Chivington ordered the killing of Confederate prisoners to prevent their recapture. In combat, he proved to be a brave fighter who fought alongside his men.

At Kozlowski's Ranch, Chivington learned that Confederates were nearby. At 2:00 a.m. on March 26, Lieutenant George Nelson of Company F (a cavalry company) of the First Colorado was sent up the Santa Fe Trail with a scouting patrol of twenty men. The patrol "roamed all the rest of the night," according to one member. About daylight, Nelson's men reached Pigeon's Ranch. Here they found the owner, Alexander Valle, an ardent Unionist, delighted to see the "Pike's Peaker's"; he told them of a Confederate patrol nearby. In fact, the four-man Rebel scout was actually east of Pigeon's Ranch, having passed by earlier. Somehow in the darkness, the two hostile patrols had passed each other without becoming aware of each other's presence. Nelson promptly turned back and soon encountered the Confederates. Anticipating relief after a long, cold night, the Rebels naturally thought that the men approaching from their own lines about 10:00 a.m. were friendly. Lieutenant John McIntyre, a Brigand from Colorado, asked if they had come to relieve them. Lieutenant Nelson said that, "Yes, we have come to relieve you of your arms," and his men threw up their weapons. Soon the embarrassed Rebels were on their way back to Colonel Chivington under guard.

The capture of the four men left Pyron's force exposed to surprise attack. The prisoners were taken to Chivington, who questioned them and then quickly got his men in motion toward the pass. Crossing over the pass, they had progressed about one and a half miles farther when they ran head on into Pyron's scouts about 2:00 p.m., to the surprise of each. These Confederates were probably some more of the Brigands who were leading Pyron's strung-out eighty-man battalion through the pass. Pyron's little battalion had probably started toward Glorieta Pass sometime about 1:00 p.m. Below the point of contact, the canyon begins to narrow and deepen, with occasional wider spots along it. This section was then known as Apache Canyon. Behind the Rebel scouts, Pyron's men were scattered, climbing up the pass, but the bulk of the Confederate force, Shropshire's two hundred men, were still snoozing in the warm sun around Johnson's Ranch three miles away. The scouts hurried back to their respective commands to warn them of the impeding collision with hostile armed men.

As news of the enemy's presence reached them, the Pike's Peakers, "all anxious for a fight," threw off their extra equipment and clothing and rushed forward at the "double quick" for a sight of the enemy. About one and a half miles farther on, they found the Rebels deployed across a relatively wide space in the canyon. There weren't many of them, but they had two small (six-pound) artillery pieces with them that would prove to be the Rebels' salvation that day. Over them defiantly waved a "Lone Star" flag, or as a Yankee described it, a "rag on a pole, a red flag emblazoned with the emblem of which Texas has small reason to be proud."

Apache Canyon, 1880. *Courtesy of the Museum of New Mexico.*

Pyron's men didn't hold long. Chivington—who, though a rank amateur, seems to have had natural military talent—quickly deployed his superior force so that it overlapped the Confederates on both ends of their line. His men worked their way up the canyon walls on both sides, overlapping the Rebels and threatening to surround them. The little cannons barked defiantly but did little real damage. The two officers assigned to command the guns, expecting no immediate trouble, had remained in Santa Fe to oversee some equipment repairs. The guns were manned by three inexperienced noncommissioned officers and some volunteers. They fired too high to be effective, but it confused many of the novice Colorado troops and caused Captain George Howland's company of U.S. Regular Cavalry (Third U.S. Cavalry) to break in confusion when their horses proved unmanageable—or when the troops were overcome by fear, depending on the observer's opinion.

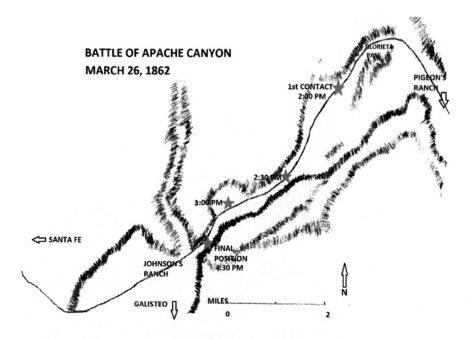

The Battle of Apache Canyon, March 26, 1862.

Chivington soon reestablished control and threatened to overwhelm the game little Confederate force.

Pyron understood when enough was enough and extricated his forces at full speed to a more defensible portion, one and a half miles farther into the canyon at a narrow point. This meant that the guns had to be limbered up for the retreat and couldn't fire. Anticipating this, Captain Howland's company had been ordered by Chivington to charge the guns whenever the Rebels retreated. It failed to act, and the guns made a clean getaway even though the Rebels had to stop for a time to repair the wheel of one piece. Officers of the other cavalry companies also stood around like "Stoughton bottles" and did nothing. "We had no head," one of the Union troopers complained.

Pyron's men retreated at a gallop for nearly a mile and a half until they began to meet Shropshire's men. Together, they turned to create a new defensive position in a narrow place in the canyon. It had finally warmed up enough by noon for Shropshire's men to get comfortably asleep. As veteran Bill Davidson later remembered, suddenly "we were rudely awakened from our slumber by a volley of musketry." Although caught by surprise—they thought that the Brigands were on guard—they reacted quickly:

> *In a moment every fellow was on his feet, gun in hand, to repel the assailants. It was reported that the enemy was about to capture the cannons. Everything was in confusion, but every fellow put out at his best speed for our cannon…*[When they met Pyron's troops,] *coming to us with the cannon at full speed we heaved a sigh of relief. The two leaders, Pyron and Shropshire, rapidly moved back and forth, calm, cool and deliberately restoring order and forming us in line to meet the foe and we finally succeeded. The companies, however, in picking their camping ground were considerably scattered, and while each* [company] *was fighting all the time upon their own hook, yet it took a considerable time to get them together in order to have some concert of action.*

Pyron placed his own troops, including the Brigands and the two artillery pieces, in the canyon bottom across the trail. He put two of Shropshire's companies on each flank on the higher ground. The left flank rested on a steep, rocky hillside that looked to observers like a castle or a fortress wall. The right rested on another steep hillside.

Chivington cautiously followed the retreating Rebels down into the canyon. He found them waiting for him in "another and more advantageous position, completely covering the sides of the mountain with their skirmishers to support their guns in the canyon below them." Chivington deployed Company D on the right and Companies A and E, of the Colorado Volunteers, on the left; dismounting his cavalry to fight as infantry, he put them into the center. Company F, a cavalry company under Captain Sam Cook, remained mounted as a reserve under strict orders to charge the Confederates "the moment they gave way." On the other side, the Rebels had managed to create a stable defensive position after some initial confusion, Captain Denman Shannon with Company C of Shropshire's battalion deployed too far forward. They soon found themselves trapped in a pocket and had to fight their way out with a loss of sixteen prisoners. The small fight raged for nearly an hour. Pyron's command not only stopped the Union advance, but they had also begun to push the Federals back on the Confederate right flank when disaster struck.

The disaster came in the form of Captain Jacob Downing's, D Company, First Colorado Volunteers, which suddenly appeared behind the Confederates. Downing, a New York–born lawyer and probate judge from Denver, had recruited his company from the Denver streets and the tough miners in the mountain camps. His men had worked their way around a small hill on the Rebel left to come in behind Pyron's lines. Pyron, a tough, aggressive veteran of the Mexican-American War, reacted immediately. He ordered Shropshire's men to form a new defensive line across a north-facing canyon that ran into the main canyon from the south, across from where Downing's company was threatening. The remaining troops successfully headed on the "skedaddle" back toward Johnson's Ranch.

Somehow, in the confusion, Company A, Major Shropshire's original company "didn't get the word" and found itself isolated and encircled by the Yankees. Shropshire saw the plight of his former command. "Like an avalanche he came to us right through the lines of the enemy," one survivor recalled. He was "grand, mighty and magnificent," as he led most of his company to safety. Some twenty-seven men were lost here, killed or captured. The Confederates eventually regrouped near Johnson's Ranch.

The retreat had been accelerated by a Federal cavalry charge that had finally occurred. When none of the Regular U.S. Cavalry companies appeared eager to charge the Confederates, Captain Sam Cook volunteered his Company F for the task. They were too late to be decisive; the Rebel cannons were long gone, but the Colorado cavalrymen charged four abreast some eight hundred yards down the narrow canyon against fire from the scattered and retreating Rebels, some of whom they captured. In writing of it later, Chivington imaginatively turned the charge into a heroic attack under heavy fire, leaping a deep ravine and slaughtering Confederates, none of which occurred.

Darkness came early that day, but not early enough for the Confederates, who fearfully awaited a renewal of the Federal onslaught. Chivington, whose objectives that day are unclear, had had enough and turned his soldiers back over the pass to Pigeon's Ranch. Pyron, desperate for time to reorganize his shattered command and hoping for reinforcements, seized the opportunity. He sent staff officers toward Union lines asking for a truce to allow both sides to tend the wounded and bury the dead. His real motive was to buy enough time to be reinforced by Scurry's command, now at Galisteo, fifteen miles away. The Confederate truce party had to ride long and hard to catch up with the Yankees to arrange the overnight truce. Both sides had retreated from the battlefield.

Casualties on both sides were light by Civil War standards, except for the seventy-one Confederates taken prisoners, some 25 percent of Pyron's command. The Federals lost five killed (four of the deaths resulted from Cook's cavalry charge), eleven to fourteen wounded and three men captured. The Rebels had an unknown number wounded (only one is recorded) and three dead. One of the dead was Private Thomas Cater of the Brigands. The Irish-born Cater, who had been mustered into Confederate service in Santa Fe on March 21, 1862, must have had one of the shortest (five days) military careers in history.

Pyron's situation by the evening of March 26, 1862, was truly grim. He sent a courier galloping toward Galisteo, where Scurry's column was expected to be awaiting juncture with the Third TMV. The tired and hungry troops were just setting up camp on Beard Ranch when they saw the dust cloud raised by the racing courier. He handed Pyron's message to Scurry between 4:00 p.m. and 5:00 p.m.: "Col. The enemy has moved down from Fort Union and is in full force in my front, and we had heavy skirmishes during the day. I have a strong position. Will hold them at bay, and wait your arrival."

A soldier remembered, "All was bustle and confusion in a moment and soon we are on the way to their relief, meat in one hand, and bread in the other, eating as we go, gun and blankets on our back." The troops had just been issued rations: sheep on the hoof, "old and poor." Some of "the ewes were so near lambing that the lambs were taken from them alive" when they were slaughtered. But it was more and better food than they had had for days, and they were eagerly anticipating their supper. Few got much as Scurry led his already tired men as fast as they could march through the night toward Johnson's Ranch. They hoped to be in time to save Pyron's beleaguered little force from the Yankee attacks that they expected when morning came. It was a hard twelve-mile march for tired men. When the horses faltered, the men had to drag the artillery over and down a mountain with long ropes. They arrived about 3:00 a.m. to the great joy of Pyron's soldiers. Scrounging in the darkness for firewood, the men built large fires and gathered around them, talking about the exciting events of the day. Some were able to sleep or find food as they awaited dawn and the expected Union assault. When there was enough daylight, Scurry and Pyron led their men to a narrow, defensible part of the canyon near Johnson's Ranch, emplaced their artillery, threw up crude fortifications and waited.

But no Yankee attack came that day. Chivington, like Pyron, had pulled his troops back to rest and await reinforcements at Kozlowski's Ranch, where there was adequate water for his men and animals. Both commanders recognized that they had met and fought only the advance guard of their enemy, and neither knew exactly what was behind it. Hearing of the action at Apache Canyon, Colonel John Slough hurried to reinforce Chivington with the remainder of his force. They left Bernal Springs at noon on March 27 and reached Kozlowski's between 2:00 a.m. and 3:00 a.m. on March 28. The scenes of a joyous reunion of forces mirrored the Confederate celebration of a day before when Scurry had arrived at Johnson's Ranch. Slough allowed his tired men only a few hours of rest before he pressed on toward Santa Fe.

Slough left Kozlowski's Ranch about 9:00 a.m. with 1,342 men. Three miles from Kozlowski's, Colonel Chivington turned southwest onto a road that provided a shortcut about six miles across Glorieta Mesa to Galisteo. Thinking that the Rebels were still near Johnson's Ranch, Slough intended to attack through Glorieta Pass, while Chivington with more than one-third of the Union strength (518 men) would fall decisively on the Confederate rear. A detachment of 40 men of the Third U.S. Cavalry was dispatched to scout farther south toward Galisteo and watch for the remaining Confederate forces under Colonel Tom Green, which weren't actually coming. With the remaining 800 men and all of the artillery (eight guns), Slough arrived at Pigeon's Ranch about 9:30 a.m. There he found

The terrain fought over at Glorieta. *Courtesy of Mike Werve.*

to his horror that his scouts (Regular U.S. Cavalry), who he thought were picketing Glorieta Pass, were enjoying a late breakfast. When they had not been relieved at dawn, as expected, the videttes had simply abandoned their posts and returned to Pigeon's Ranch. Slough hurriedly sent scouts toward the pass while his men rested and filled their canteens. The scouts only proceeded three to six hundred yards when they ran headlong into the Brigands, the vanguard of Scurry's force coming toward them. One of the Coloradans shouted, "Get out of our way you damned sons of b-s. We are going to take dinner in Santa Fe." William Kirk of the Brigands yelled back, "You'll take dinner in Hell," and "the jig opened." Some of the scouts quickly returned to their respective commanders with their warning of nearby foes, while others skirmished warily.

Scurry, never a patient man, had waited impatiently all day, March 27, for a Yankee attack that never came. But now on Friday, March 28, he moved out with almost his entire command and headed up the canyon from Johnson's Ranch, looking for a fight. With six to seven hundred men and three light artillery pieces, he headed through Glorieta Pass, toward an enemy of unknown strength, in an unknown location and for unclear tactical or strategic ends. Scurry's (and Slough's) ignorance of his opponents' disposition points to a curious feature of the Glorieta campaign: the failure of either side to carry out an effective reconnaissance even though both had plenty of high-quality cavalry available. Thus, at 10:00 a.m. on March 28, 1862, both sides were surprised when their main bodies collided a mile from Pigeon's Ranch. Slough's amateur plans had come completely unraveled. The flanking force, under Chivington, representing one-third of his strength, was half a day's march away and unaware of the situation. A Confederate force nearly equal to his own was suddenly at close quarters, moving aggressively against him. On the other hand, there is no evidence that Scurry had any plans that morning other than to seek out his enemy and fight him. Scurry quickly recovered his equilibrium, but Slough never fully did.

When he realized that the Yankees weren't coming to him, Scurry went to them. He took his entire command except for a small train guard (perhaps about 30 men) that he left at Johnson's Ranch with one small cannon. There were also about 170 other "casuals" at the ranch, mostly noncombatants, sick and wounded, hospital staff and (mostly) teamsters, some of whom were civilians. The 600 to 700 fighting men with Scurry came from nine companies of the Fourth TMV, four companies of the Seventh and four companies of the Fifth, as well as the Brigands and some other irregulars. Scurry also had three pieces of artillery, two of his own guns and one of Pyron's, all commanded by Lieutenant James Bradford. The two twelve-pound howitzers that Scurry brought with his column had been captured from the Yankees at Valverde.

The forces that collided at Pigeon's Ranch were fairly closely matched. Slough enjoyed an advantage of 884 to 600–700 men, with six companies of the First Colorado and three companies of Regular cavalry (two from the Third U.S. and one from the First). His dominant artillery had eight guns (two twelve-pounders, two six-pounders and four twelve-pound mountain howitzers) organized in two batteries. Yet throughout the day the Rebels would enjoy numerical superiority at the critical points: on

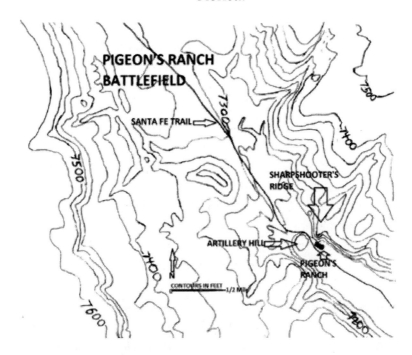

The Pigeon's Ranch battlefield.

the flanks. Slough, untrained and inexperienced as a soldier, kept nearly one-third of his force tied down as reserves, train guards and so on. Most of the remainder were concentrated in the center of his line in the canyon. Scurry, by contrast, had fought with distinction as an officer in the Mexican-American War. The Rebels were able to constantly force the flanks of successive Union positions as the Union companies were defeated in detail. They failed, however, to crack the Union center. Despite this success at concentrating their troops where they were needed most, the lack of train guards at Johnson's Ranch would later come to haunt the Army of New Mexico.

Taken initially by surprise at the nearness of the enemy, the Rebels hastily prepared to fight. "We did some of the fastest forming of our lives," one veteran remembered. Dismounting the men on horseback and putting them into line with the infantry, as well as placing Bradford's three guns on a little rise in the middle of the valley, Scurry's men quickly formed a line of battle across the canyon that lapped up onto the wooded slopes on both flanks. They were in position when the advance guard of Slough's force, a company of Regular cavalry, reached them. Bradford immediately opened fire. Scurry had sent Pyron and his men to the Confederate right. Major Henry Raguet commanded the center and also took charge of the left. Surprised and shocked by the sudden barrage from Bradford's guns, Slough's men did some hasty forming themselves.

When they had arrived at Pigeon's Ranch, the men of the First Colorado had stacked their weapons and then wandered off, filling their canteens, making fires for coffee and so on. When the Rebel cannons fired, "the boys had to run several hundred yards to get to there [sic] guns," one soldier witness reported. "That was a fool-hardy trick." Slough's scouts had already formed a skirmish line, to which he added both artillery batteries, the infantry and (dismounted) cavalry as they hurried forward. Slough attempted to emulate Chivington's tactics of two days earlier and pushed troops up into the high ground on either flank. However, he used too small a force, a single company on each flank, which the Rebels eventually contained and then pushed back. Then they, in turn, threatened to envelop the Union center, where the bulk of Slough's committed troops were supporting the artillery.

On the Confederate right, Pyron's men were threatened by Captain Jacob Downing's Company D, of the First Colorado, which was attempting to repeat its success at Apache Canyon when it had flanked Pyron's men by passing along a wooded hillside around a small hill to get to their rear. This time the Rebels controlled the high ground in the trees and forced Company D into the open, where the men suffered numerous casualties. Among them was an unlucky young Colorado miner turned soldier, Jesse Haire, who was captured. A diminutive youngster, Haire had been made the drummer of Company D despite his lack of musical training. As a musician, he drummed during drills instead of practicing soldiery skills. In Glorieta Canyon, there was little need for music and, besides, "some rascal of a Reble [sic] shot a hole through my drum and knocked one of my ebeny [sic] sticks a hundred feet out of my hands." So he fought in the line of battle. Cut off amidst the Texans in the trees, Haire fought an individual duel with a Texan, each behind a tree, until he ran out of ammunition and surrendered. His captors were greatly amused when they found Haire's cartridge box half full. He never knew there were *two* layers of cartridges in the cartridge box and surrendered when the top layer ran out.

Shropshire soon detected a Union force moving to turn the Confederate left. He warned Pyron, who, believing his own position secure after repulsing Downing's Company D, decided to warn Scurry personally. As he galloped in the open across the canyon, a well-aimed Union artillery shell took off his horse's head, tumbling horse and rider in a bloody heap. Unperturbed, Pyron pulled his pistols from their saddle holsters and hurried on toward the north end of the Rebel line.

Here, Company I of the First Colorado, a German company commanded by Lieutenant Charles Kerber, was sent by Slough to outflank that end of the Rebel lines. Spying a gully that ran west and could provide a covered path around the Texans' flank, the I company soldiers tried to sneak along it, out of sight of the Rebels. But they were seen, and soon an assault force of Fourth and Seventh TMV troopers raced two hundred yards across the open ground, exposed to Union crossfire, to fall on the men in the gully. It was vicious, close fighting. Captain Charles Buckholtz of the Fourth TMV killed two men with a knife after he emptied his pistol. The shotguns of the Texans did effective work at these close quarters. Witnesses described how Ben White of the Fourth fought:

> *White took a handful of powder, poured it into one barrel of his gun, took another handful, poured in into the other barrel, put a little paper on it and rammed down and then poured a handful of shot in each barrel, ran a little paper down and turned both barrels loose right down that ravine and killed and wounded at least ten of them and scared the balance of them to death.*

The survivors fled in disorder. They made another stand in another shallow gully and, when driven from it, fell back to a steep, rocky hillside, where they held for a time.

The fighting was fiercest on the two hillside flanks. The hillsides were thickly wooded, mostly with cedar, and the battle became one of "the bushwacking kind," as Coloradoans fought Texans in a hundred little individual fights. A Rebel private remembered that "the country was so rough, the pine and cedar so thick, that the companies and men all got mixed up before we had been fighting very long."

In thick cover and dense gun smoke that hung in the valley, soldiers could only tell where the battle lines were by the sounds of firing. In the canyon and trees, this was not always a reliable guide, and more than one soldier went dangerously astray in the trees. Gathering up whatever men they could find of whatever unit, the Confederate officers personally led their soldiers forward through the thickets in point-blank combat. In the process, they incurred horrendous casualties. Every Confederate field officer at Pigeon's Ranch was either killed, wounded or captured on this day of battle. Significantly, only three Union officers were wounded in combat. One of them, lying helpless on the battlefield, was beaten to death by civilian looters during the night. Perhaps even more significantly, the Northern officers were under orders to neither carry nor use guns.

The pressure on the flanks continued, and Slough was forced to fall back three to four hundred yards to a final position in front of Pigeon's Ranch about noon. In contrast to the flanks, in the center of the valley Union forces held strong, repulsing Confederate advances. Most of Slough's strength was concentrated here, including his eight artillery pieces that were well served. Their heavier metal and accuracy wreaked havoc with the three Confederate light guns. A gunner was killed, Lieutenant Bradford (commanding) was wounded and several horses were killed. The surviving crews cut out the dead horses and fell back down the canyon. Upon hearing his guns fall silent, Scurry angrily rushed to the scene and brought them back into action with "volunteer" crews gathered nearby.

Slough's new position was a strong one, anchored on the adobe walls of the corrals at Pigeon's Ranch and on hills to the north and south. Slough sent Lieutenant Colonel Samuel Tappan to the south to hold a key terrain feature known later as Artillery Hill after he had pointed out its tactical importance to Slough. From the high ground, Tappan could see two to three hundred Confederates forming a mile away for an attack. Slough gave him only twenty men, but Tappan recognized the

Sharpshooter's Ridge and the last remaining structure at Pigeon's Ranch, 2011.

critical importance of holding the high ground that dominated Pigeon's Ranch and the Santa Fe Trail east of the ranch, which was the Union line of retreat. He also recognized the inadequacy of the force Slough assigned, and so he gathered up about one hundred more men from underutilized rear echelon troops such as police and train guards, as well as any stragglers he could find, to reinforce the troops already there. Lieutenant Ira Claflin's battery of twelve-pound howitzers was sent in support. To the north of the ranch, a high, narrow ridge jutted south toward the ranch buildings that it overlooked. It was a naturally strong position, with a steep, rocky face toward the Rebels to the west. Known today as Sharpshooter's Ridge, it proved to be the decisive terrain feature of the battle.

Meanwhile, Scurry was gathering his scattered forces and trying to organize them for an assault on the Union position. It was about 1:00 p.m. before he renewed the assault. He was able to bring two artillery pieces, the two twelve-pound guns, back on line. From his position, Scurry was unable to determine where the enemy's main lines were: either along the ranch wall or farther back along a rocky ledge above the Ranch. So he pushed forward the two light guns to develop the enemy position. Unfortunately for them, the Rebel gunners soon located the Union battery behind the corral walls. In a remarkable display of accurate shooting, the Union artillerymen dismounted one of the Rebel guns with a direct hit on the muzzle and blew up the caisson of the other, putting both out of action. Without artillery support and facing larger Union forces behind good cover, supported by its own excellently served artillery, Scurry's repeated attacks on the Union center got nowhere and simply piled up Rebel casualties.

Scurry had planned attacks on both flanks to coincide with his own in the center. The assault on the right flank was probably intended by Scurry to be his decisive thrust. A successful attack over or around Artillery Hill would have put the Rebels astride the Santa Fe Trail, the Union line of retreat. To attack Tappan's men on Artillery Hill, he sent Major John Shropshire with three companies of the Seventh TMV, along with some scattered troops he gathered up—in all about 120 men. Tappan had between 220 and 240 men to defend the hill and a well-served four-gun battery of artillery. Shropshire's attack miscarried in the thick cedar brush of the west side of Artillery Hill. He had aimed to swing around the southern flanks of the hill, where the slope was lower and a gap offered a route around it to the Santa Fe Trail. Shropshire's men soon were tangled in the maze of cedar and piñon, and their attack degenerated into a series of small skirmishes in the thick cover. Rallying their men and personally leading them forward, Shropshire was killed and Captain Denman Shannon captured. Their disheartened men fell back. Eventually, to restore the situation, Scurry had to take personal command on the right. By then Tappan's men had retreated from the hill.

Shropshire's route had led his men along the base of Artillery Hill to the south. The movement had opened a wide gap between the Confederate center and right. Into this gap wandered soldier-artist-lawyer-diarist Sergeant A.B. Peticolas of the Fourth TMV, through the thick trees and battle smoke, where he got lost:

I was in the extreme left of the charging party and in fact on the very verge of the hill. The undergrowth was thick and I did not see that Major Shropshire, Captain Buckholts, and 3 men had been killed by the firing I heard on my right, nor hear that Scurry had ordered the men to fall back. The men having obliqued to the right, so that when I ceased [advancing], I thought that the enemy had been forced back by our

[men] *and that they had taken out toward the hills, as I thought the firing seemed to tend in that direction. So not desiring to follow in that direction, but having an excellent chance to fire across in the valley at the artillerymen and on the left, I began to take part in the battle again by walking leisurely along the hill towards where their line was, firing at every opportunity down at the enemy. I was thus slowly advancing and after having fired ½ dozen shots thus, was loading my gun when on turning ½ around, and to my astonishment, saw that I was in two feet of a line of 100 men, all strangers to me. Another glance as I returned ramming convinced me that they were Pikes Peakers and in a moment I thought, well, I'm a prisoner after all. Here are the enemy. Before I could act upon this conviction; in fact before I had decided what to do with 50 men looking at me and possessing the power to riddle me with pistol balls or minie balls or plunge a bayonet in me—the major* [Lieutenant Colonel Tappan] *of the enemy nearest me, a man with a red band cap, dark eyes and whiskers and rather handsome face, height 5ft 10 in., said looking straight into my face, "you had better look out, Captain, or those fellows will shoot you."* [Peticolas was wearing a captured Union uniform overcoat] *Now though I knew that he referred to our men and mistook me for some on his own side, I felt puzzled to say anything save to look inquiringly at him and ask, "Who will?" my voice did not betray that 50 men were looking at me and none of them by word or sign showed that he knew me in my true character. He answered, "Why, those fellows over yonder," pointing in the direction of our boys. "There are two or three of them over there shooting at us." "Is there," said I; "Then I'll go over that way and take a shot at them." I started off with my gun at charge bayonets, walking cautiously, taking advantage of the trees as if advancing on a real foe, and as I thus walked off, I looked anew over my shoulder at the man who had been talking to me. He was watching me very closely and I felt some uneasiness lest he shoot me in the back as I went off, but his honest eyes look no suspicion, and in a dozen steps further I was out of sight and over in our own lines once more.*

Repulsed in the center and the right flank, the Confederates finally succeeded on their left in turning the strong Federal position. Here,

Major Henry Raguet of the Fourth TMV—with almost 120 men and Pyron's 80 men, including Brigands—steadily drove the three companies of Pike's Peakers and Regulars back in desperate close-quarter fighting, which raged throughout the afternoon. Raguet was killed in the point-blank combat, and his infuriated men stormed into the Union defenders. Pyron's men, meanwhile, worked their way to higher ground at the north end of the Union line, which put them in a position in which they were able to flank each successive Union defensive position above Sharpshooter's Ridge. The bluecoats fought hard and stubbornly, giving their artillery and infantry sufficient time to retreat down the Santa Fe Trail to safety before their position collapsed and they fled precipitously. Slough had already chosen another defensive position about one mile down the trail from Pigeon's Ranch, where there was open ground for

Pigeon's Ranch, 1880. *Courtesy of the Museum of New Mexico.*

his artillery and his flanks were securely anchored on high ground. No one thought to tell Lieutenant Colonel Lewis Tappan about the retreat. He was nearly cut off by the Confederate advance, but he recognized the situation in time and led his men "by circuitous route" to the new defensive line, avoiding the Rebels. As dusk fell and Scurry's men reached the new Union line, Scurry attempted to mount another attack, but the gathering darkness, the lethal and undamaged Union artillery and their own exhaustion soon put an end to the halfhearted effort. The Rebels fell back to Pigeon's Ranch, and then they realized that Slough was pulling out and retreating.

Scurry's men had won a hard-fought tactical victory over a better-armed enemy of about equal numbers. The casualties suffered by both sides at the battles at Glorieta were heavy (10–15 percent) but not horrendous by Civil War standards. The Federals suffered forty-seven killed, eighty-three wounded and eleven prisoners. The Southerners lost forty-four dead, sixty-three wounded and thirty-one taken

Johnson's Ranch at Apache Canyon, 2011.

prisoner. The Union soldiers fought as well as the Rebels, but Slough's faulty tactical dispositions doomed their efforts. Slough, expecting Chivington's men to fall on the Confederate rear at any moment, had remained on the defensive all day. At the end of the day, the Rebels held the battleground, the traditional litmus test of victory. It was a fruitless victory, however—Slough's force was intact and reunited and still stood between the Confederates and Fort Union, to which they could always retreat and which was impregnable to the Rebels with their limited resources. Somewhere to the south, Canby lurked with the main Union army that was rumored to have left Fort Craig. Even as they celebrated their hard-won victory, the more clearheaded realized that "that [they] were in a hell of a fix." And that was before they learned of the disaster that had struck their trains at Johnson's Ranch.

Slough had anticipated that the Rebels were near Johnson's Ranch, where he expected to encounter them. He sent Major John Chivington with 518 men, one-third of his strength, on a wide flanking movement six miles across Glorieta Mesa to the south to fall on them there while he moved against them down the canyon. But Scurry didn't behave

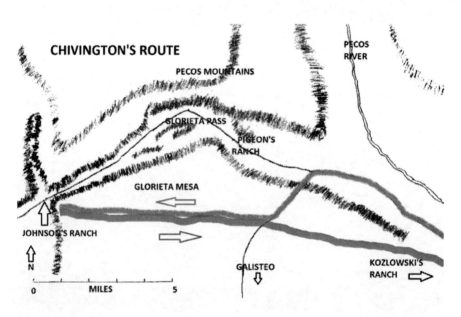

Chivington's route across Glorieta Mesa.

according to Slough's script and instead aggressively came after him with his whole force. They collided at Pigeon's Ranch. Meanwhile, Chivington's flanking strike fell on air. He arrived at the six-hundred-foot cliffs overlooking Johnson's Ranch, but Scurry was nowhere in sight. What was spread out below him in the dry canyon was the wagon park of the Army of New Mexico, with only a small (30 men) train guard, as well as the sick and wounded. Lieutenant Colonel Manuel Chavez (New Mexico Volunteers) guided Chivington's column across the mesa. Now he pointed into the canyon and told the colonel, "You are on top of them." Chavez had remained with the colors when most of his men deserted. After waiting more than two hours for Slough, Chivington finally decided to destroy the trains, which he did with few casualties to either side.

Chivington learned from some Union prisoners he had recaptured that Slough was being beaten in Glorieta Canyon and hastened to return after dark across Glorieta Mesa by a route that avoided contact with the Rebels. He rejoined Slough at Kozlowski's Ranch. The serendipitous destruction of the army's wagon train by Chivington essentially brought the campaign of the Army of New Mexico in the West to an end, although the Rebel high command was slow to recognize the full import of its predicament and Federal leaders even slower. The destruction was complete. The loss included most of the food supply of the army, most of the wagons, almost all of the soldiers' personal belongings, ammunition and three hundred to six hundred horses and mules. The army would never again have enough ammunition, particularly for the artillery, to fight a major battle, nor enough horses and mules to move even the remaining wagons and guns. The victorious army, in fact, faced imminent danger from cold and hunger and needed to fall back to Santa Fe to survive. Many of the wounded wouldn't make it.

Scurry's men at Pigeon's Ranch needed a truce, and they needed it quickly. Scurry looked around him for something to use as a white flag. "God damn it, tear off your shirt tail, we have got to have a white flag," he ordered those around him. He wanted to "send a flag of truce to tell them damned Yankees to come back and pick up their dead and wounded." No one had anything white enough to serve. Finally, a private reluctantly pulled out a luxurious white silk handkerchief that he had just found on the battlefield. Then he sadly watched it ride away with Pyron and Major Alexander Jackson toward Union lines, correctly suspecting that he would never see it again. The Rebel delegation had to ride hard and far to catch up with the retreating Federals, who retreated first to Kozlowski's Ranch, then to Bernal Springs and finally to Fort Union. Each army was eager to distance itself from the other. Behind them they left a valley filled with dead and wounded horses and men. Soon, parties of men from both armies returned to range over the battlefield in the darkness, looking for the bodies of the dead and the still living with improvised torches. When the hostile burial parties met, they treated each other with elaborate courtesy, as had happened at Valverde. Learning that the Rebels had lost all of their entrenching tools at Johnson's Ranch, the Yankees lent them sufficient shovels and picks to complete the sad task of burial. They also generously shared their own medical supplies, ordered more from Fort Union and then shared those.

When it was clear that the Union forces were not going to interfere, Scurry's men were able to retire. There were no supplies left for the Confederate survivors who fell back to Johnson's Ranch from the Pigeon's Ranch battlefield late the next day, neither food nor blankets nor medicine. Their only choice was to return quickly to Santa Fe. Many of the wounded couldn't be moved and were left in whatever makeshift shelter could be found or created. The rest, exhausted and freezing, stumbled in the darkness toward town. Many simply quit alongside the road, built fires and waited for a better day. It didn't look like a victorious army that straggled into Santa Fe, seeking shelter and food where there was little to be had. The condition of the wounded was particularly pitiable. They lacked medicine, food, blankets and shelter, and there weren't enough wagons and mules left to move them from Johnson's Ranch to town.

At this point, an angel intervened in the unlikely form of Mrs. Louisa Canby, Union general Canby's wife, who had remained in Santa Fe. Touched to tears by the suffering of the wounded young Confederate soldiers, Mrs. Canby organized the women of Santa Fe to provide food, blankets and care. She took many into her own "large home," nursing as many as fourteen at a time. And it was Louisa Canby who devised a scheme to move the painfully wounded from the battlefield using tent halves to make hammocks on wagon frames. When she realized that the Rebel soldiers were near freezing for lack of blankets and clothes, she revealed the secret walled-in hiding place of treaty goods originally meant for the Navajos, now on the warpath. Daily she rode out to the wounded who couldn't be moved, bringing them nourishment and comfort. Louisa Canby was "loved and her memory cherished" by the survivors of the Army of New Mexico in a way no other woman ever was during the war and long afterward.

Across the mountains, Colonel Slough retreated out of the war. Shaken by his defeat and the near disaster at Pigeon's Ranch, and not yet understanding the implications of Chivington's raid, Slough also was facing possible charges for disobeying Canby's orders and precipitating a major battle. He resigned his commission, passing command of the First Colorado to Chivington and overall command to Colonel Paul. Under new leadership, the defeatist gloom quickly dissipated as the troops learned more about Chivington's attack and the retreat of the Rebels to Santa Fe. Soon they were eager to be at the Texans again.

Chapter 7

After Glorieta

At Fort Craig, Canby had been following events with growing alarm. Anticipating Slough's defeat, he prepared to take the field and sortied on April 1. Canby took 1,210 men (860 Regulars and 350 reliable volunteers), leaving ten companies of the efficient First New Mexico under Colonel Kit Carson to hold the fort. Canby had hoped to surprise the Rebels by a rapid march on Albuquerque, but the same sand roads that had slowed Sibley's earlier advance now delayed him. Nevertheless, he arrived unexpectedly on the southeast side of Albuquerque on the afternoon of April 8, to the consternation of the tiny Rebel garrison.

Canby's men were within twenty-four miles of Albuquerque before they were detected. The earlier dominance of the Confederate cavalry, which resulted in their more effective scouting of the enemy and screening of their own forces, had withered away as thousands of horses and mules had been lost and not replaced. Also, many New Mexico troops, emboldened by events, were returning to the field, overcoming their traditional fear of the "Texians." They were much more effective operating as dispersed cavalry than they were on the battlefield and had success interrupting Confederate lines of communication and reconnaissance. Canby, understanding both the strengths and weaknesses of his New Mexico troops, used them shrewdly. Their presence severely affected Confederate operations in the latter stages of the campaign, particularly in their ability to forage through the countryside.

Canby's move caught the Confederates unprepared. Sibley seems to have thought that Canby would remain passive while he maneuvered all over the territory. When Sibley learned of the desperate condition of Scurry's men, he rushed the remainder of his forces and all the supplies they could carry to Santa Fe, leaving only a weak guard at Albuquerque. In that city, defending the last supplies the Rebels had, were only 226 men: "Gooch" Hardeman's Company A of the Fourth TMV, Captain James Walker's Company D of the Second TMV (Baylor's), about 25 men of the San Elizario Company, Captain John Reily's two light artillery pieces and the sick and wounded from the hospital, which included Captain Walker.

Canby, the skilled strategist, had multiple objectives, depending on circumstances. By threatening Albuquerque, he might be able to take the lightly defended town with small risk, but even threatening it would allow him to slip past the city through Tijeras Pass in the Sandia Mountains to join up with Colonel Paul's force approaching from Fort Union. It also would force the Rebels to abandon Santa Fe.

The tiny Confederate force had been shocked into frenetic activity by Canby's sudden appearance. They sent courier after courier to Santa Fe carrying increasingly desperate pleas for help. Meanwhile, the few troops available and Reily's guns were raced from point to point around the city's eastern perimeter as Canby alternately threatened them. They put on such a strong show of resistance that Canby never pressed home an attack, either on March 8 or 9, when he renewed his probing. Reluctant to bombard a town full of civilians, and meeting stronger than expected resistance, Canby pulled his men back toward the mountains and went into camp. On the night of April 9, they slipped away, leaving their campfires burning, to San Antonio, east of the mountains, near to the planned rendezvous with the Fort Union troops at Carnuel. Canby had achieved his minimal goals and, because of that, had forced the Rebels to take the final decision to abandon northern New Mexico. Only one man, a Union officer, was wounded in the so-called Battle of Albuquerque.

General Sibley had actually learned of Canby's preparations to leave Fort Craig from his spies, before March 25. He hurriedly sent out orders for his scattered forces to concentrate at the Village of Manzano, east of the Albuquerque and the mountains, where he might prevent a juncture of the two Union forces. The move would provide a better line of retreat or of reinforcement, if any ever came from Texas. Sibley expected that he could find food and fodder there, but this seems dubious in reality. The resources in the Albuquerque–Santa Fe area were exhausted, and his army had to go somewhere. But his aggressive subordinate, Scurry, had brought on a major battle at Glorieta before he had received Sibley's orders. Sibley was still determined to move to Manzano, and the Confederates in Santa Fe had already begun the trek back southward when Canby struck.

Pyron and most of the Second TMV left Santa Fe on April 7, and most of Tom Green's regiment (Fifth) left on the eighth. The other troops left between April 8 and 11. Their march suddenly became a desperate race to reach Albuquerque in time to save its beleaguered little garrison. One veteran of the Fourth TMV recorded the hardships of that march. After a hard day's march on April 8, they were roused from their icy beds when word of Canby's attack on Albuquerque reached them. They hurriedly formed and marched south all night, some thirty miles through snow and rain. They were given little food, and rain and snow soaked their clothes and bedding. They arrived in Albuquerque on April 11 in time to see the last of Canby's men heading through Tijeras Canyon. "Oh the suffering of this march words can never tell," one soldier remembered. Some units had barely reached Santa Fe when they turned around and marched back south. Behind them, to hold Santa Fe temporarily, they left the Brigands.

Facing Canby's now united army, the logic of their perilous state finally sank into the minds of the Confederate commanders. They could no longer fall back on Manzano. Sibley had already appealed to Richmond for reinforcements. Until they arrived with supplies, the Confederates would be unable to renew the campaign. They were also unable to maintain themselves in northern New Mexico any longer. The scanty resources, food and forage of the area had been thoroughly exhausted. Sibley soon decided that the Army of New Mexico would have to evacuate the territory. Canby had achieved a junction with the Fort Union troops at Carnuel, dangerously close to Albuquerque, and the Rebels were no longer able to fight a major battle. Their only choices were to fight under hopeless conditions or to abandon New Mexico, if they could still escape. "The course adopted was deemed the wisest," Sibley wrote to his superiors. The decision, once made, was rapidly implemented. The first troops began leaving on April 12, followed by most of the remaining ones over the next two days.

Behind them, Sibley's men left their sick and wounded (about two hundred men) in hospitals in Santa Fe, Albuquerque and Socorro. When they arrived, the Union troops had studiously avoided bothering the Rebel hospitals until they ran out of food and medical supplies and appealed for help. Then the Federals required them to formally surrender but also supplied them generously. As the sick and wounded recovered, they were paroled and sent back to Texas under escort.

In Albuquerque, Sibley's men burned the supplies they couldn't carry and the wagons for which they had no animals. Under the watchful eye of the commander of the artillery, Trevanion T. Teel, eight little mountain howitzers were secretly buried in a corral near the old plaza. The Confederates lacked ammunition for the guns and horses or mules to pull them. Some twenty-seven years later, Teel, by then a prominent attorney, directed the exhumation of the still undiscovered guns in a special ceremony before a large crowd. But in 1862, there was little of the later spirit of reconciliation in the land, and the ragtag Rebel army hurried south to escape Canby's powerful grasp. The soldiers had twenty days' worth of food left, were mostly on foot and didn't have enough ammunition left to fight a battle. They left Albuquerque at dawn on April 12. The men on foot and the slower elements crossed the Rio Grande at Atrisco and proceeded south down the west bank. The mounted men under Colonel Tom Green left April 13 and marched down the east bank, where they formed a screen for the army.

Green's mounted column made poor time in its march along the river. The heavy sand, which ran for five miles along the road, slowed their wagons, especially the heavy ox-drawn provisions wagons. The civilian wagon master stubbornly refused to allow his oxen to be hurried, despite insistent orders. Then he insisted on going into camp several miles north of Peralta, well away from the protection of Green's main force. Finally, despairing that the wagons would catch up, Green decided to camp at Peralta for the night, far short of his intended destination. The contents of the heavy wagons, mostly provisions, were loaded onto light wagons and ferried into Peralta to await the heavier ones when they were free of the sand. A company of men, with a small mountain howitzer, was left to guard the wagon train. The rest of Green's men settled down for a peaceful sleep in Peralta. But it didn't happen that way.

Peralta was a small village located on the east bank of the Rio Grande. It was also the site of the large estate of territorial governor Henry Connelley, a fabulously wealthy merchant recently appointed by President Lincoln to replace a departing Southerner. Connelley was an ardent Republican despite holding many Indian slaves himself. Connelley's estate was surrounded by a thick forest and by fields cut by acequias (irrigation ditches) and bordered with thick adobe walls. The town buildings made of adobe were impenetrable to bullets and almost impervious to artillery and were surrounded by thick-walled adobe corrals and the acequias. Peralta was the strongest natural fortification in New Mexico. Three miles south and across the flooded and rapidly rising Rio Grande was the slightly larger village of Los Lunas, where Sibley and the remainder of the army were camped. In Peralta, the tired Rebels spread their camps wherever they could, built their fires, cooked their suppers and drifted off to sleep. Some attended a fandango that lasted until the wee hours of the morning, the sound of the music drifting across the quiet fields around the village. They were clearly heard by the silently approaching men of Canby's army, which was within a few hundred yards of Peralta, undetected, and which outnumbered the Rebels by five to one.

Canby and his army had left the mountains east of Albuquerque on the morning of April 14, following Sibley. Marching hard through the day and most of the night, they made better time than Green, covering thirty-six miles, and arrived in the early morning hours. None of the Rebels had any inkling of their presence. For whatever reason, Colonel Tom Green and his staff had failed to deploy scouts to watch for Canby's approach. The first warning the Confederates had came when a valley was fired into their camp at extreme range. It was, one Texan said, "a very rude and ungentlemanly, yet very effective way of waking a fellow up." The Rebels quickly sprang to arms and took stations behind the thick adobe walls that ringed the village.

Canby and his men had been amazed at the lack of security as they approached Peralta. Quickly and quietly deployed in a wide semicircle around the village, Canby's subordinates were straining at the leash to attack the outnumbered and unsuspecting Rebels. Chivington, ever bloodthirsty, was particularly insistent on attacking before daylight. Canby, however, stubbornly refused. His stated reasons were sound: an attack in the dark, against an enemy position that had not been reconnoitered, across fields cut with unseen walls and acequias, was a recipe for disaster.

Meanwhile, just as the Union forces were deploying, a small Confederate wagon train, with a small escort, came into view. Their timing was spectacularly bad. Company F, of the First Colorado, a cavalry company, was sent after it, followed by two infantry companies. The members of the escort attempted to fight but were quickly overwhelmed by Lieutenant George Nelson's men, with the loss of six killed, three wounded and twenty-two made prisoner, as well as eighty to eighty-five mules and horses and all the wagons. Strangely, these would be almost the only Rebel casualties that day. The Northerners lost one man mortally wounded.

Green had formed his men into defensive positions behind the formidable encircling adobe walls. They were soon faced by a "dash" toward the village by the mounted company of New Mexican Scouts under the flashy Captain James "Paddy" Graydon. The New Mexicans never came close enough to the Rebel defenses to either inflict or suffer any damage and, after emptying their guns, rapidly rode off. To anchor his left, Green sent Pyron and four small companies of the Second TMV. Green himself remained in command of most of the Fifth TMV near the center of his lines. Bethel Coopwood and the San Elizario Company garrisoned the right center of the Confederate line, and there was a company of the Fifth on the extreme right. The Brigands, mounted on the best horses in the army, hovered in front of and south of the right flanks of the army, from the Rio Grande to the mountains, three to five miles. Here they formed a connecting link between Green's men in Peralta and the main force in Los Lunas. A usually reliable witness at Los Lunas reported that they numbered one hundred men. If his count is accurate, then the Brigands had been reinforced. This may indicate the presence on the battlefield of the company of Hispanic volunteers (about thirty men), commanded by Pablo C. Alderete, who are known to have been in the region and to have joined Sibley about this time. This would mark the only battle in which a unit of native New Mexicans took part on the Confederate side.

The bulk of the Union forces under Colonel Paul attempted to turn the Confederate left, slipping through the bosque along the river to cut the Rebels off from the river. They were spotted by two Confederate observers high in a church tower, and a two-gun section of light guns was rushed to support Pyron. A bloodless and fruitless artillery duel between the two guns and four heavier Union pieces lasted nearly an hour before the Northerners gave up probing the Confederate left and turned their attention to the Confederate center, where another nearly harmless artillery duel was in progress. The Confederate artillery had a great advantage in being able to fire from the shelter of thick adobe walls. However, it had two great disadvantages: it was outnumbered four light guns to the Unionists' eighteen light and heavy, and the Rebels were almost out of ammunition. The Rebels had "neither grape, shell or canister" for their guns and had only solid shot, which was of limited us against troops in the open field. Furthermore, the Rebels were too short of small arms ammunition to fight a real battle and could only fight on the defensive. As Canby refused to risk his men in an attack across the acequias cut ground, a stalemate resulted. All day long the two sides exchanged artillery fire without much effect. The Confederates suffered only one man wounded. On the other side, the light Confederate guns, firing only solid shot at long intervals, did little harm, killing four Union soldiers and a few mules. As one Union soldier remembered, "It was the most harmless battle on record."

About 11:00 a.m., Scurry, with the Fourth and Seventh TMV, arrived in Peralta to relieve Green's outnumbered troops. They had to wade several hundred yards across the flooded river, which was shoulder deep, through ice four inches thick in addition to slush. They arrived with frozen clothes and without their commander. Sibley and his staff, riding ahead of Scurry's men, crossed the Rio Grande north of Peralta. There they ran into Union cavalry and hastily recrossed the river under fire, returning to Los Lunas. Thus, for the fourth and final time that they fought an armed engagement, the Army of New Mexico did not have its commander on the field. With Scurry's arrival, there was little chance that the Union forces could overrun the strong natural position at Peralta without prohibitive losses. The Yankees, however, continued to demonstrate at various points along the line without pressing an attack home.

Near noon, Canby shifted most of his artillery to the Confederate right and massed his troops in front of the section defended by Coopwood and the San Elizario Company, the weakest-held section. It was soon obvious to Colonel Paul, who was waiting to lead the attack, that Confederate fire was slackening. His men were eager to attack what they saw as a vulnerable enemy. Paul pressed Canby for permission to attack. Canby refused. The attack turned into another desultory and bloodless artillery duel, and finally, at about 2:00 p.m., Canby ended the artillery bombardment and pulled his men back out of the range of Confederate guns.

At about this time, midafternoon, nature took over. The strong wind that had blown all day turned into an intense windstorm from the southwest. With near hurricane strength or more, the wind drove sand and dust clouds so that men and animals could neither see nor breathe in it. The combatants, who had already ceased most active operations, sought shelter wherever they could find it. The Battle of Peralta then ended, like in the words of the poet T.S. Eliot, "not with a bang but a whimper," in a sandstorm.

Many, probably most, of Canby's officers and men had been growing increasingly frustrated and angry as their commander had failed to press an attack on what they saw as a crippled and trapped Rebel army. At the time, Canby wrote that he had failed to attack on the fifteenth because he wasn't ready. His men hadn't been fed in thirty-five hours, there had been no reconnaissance of the Rebel positions and his trains had not yet caught up with the army. Canby intended to attack, he wrote, on the sixteenth, only the Confederates slipped away across the river that night.

There were growing suspicions, however, among the soldiers that Canby never really intended to attack.

In Los Lunas, General Sibley realized the gravity of his position. While Peralta provided a strong defensive position, his army lacked enough ammunition for a battle. Surrounded on three sides by a superior army with a flooded river behind them, and another enemy force athwart their lives of communication, the Confederate Army of New Mexico was again in deep trouble. Even before darkness covered the battlefield, Colonel Tom Green began preparations for a secret withdrawal across the river on Sibley's orders. The wagons, for which there were still mules, were gathered near the river. The rest, plus a lot of equipment and supplies, were simply abandoned. About 8:00 p.m., they began to cross the wagons over the Rio Grande, which was rising rapidly. The broken-down mules proved too weak to pull the wagons through the soft quicksand bottom of the flooding river awash with slush ice. Men had to jump in and remain in the freezing water, pushing the wagons across by brute force. Behind them in Peralta, campfires blazed in empty camps, and sentries marched in front of them to fool Canby's scouts. By 6:00 a.m. on April 16, all of the men and wagons were at Los Lunas, with all tired, cold and hungry but, for the moment, safe.

Sibley had stolen a day's march. Canby was surprised by the move but soon had his own forces in motion along the east bank after the Rebels. Sibley's men left Los Lunas early on April 16, with Pyron and Scurry's mounted men bringing up the rear. A Rebel diarist noted "that confounded cavalry of the enemy" dogged the column from behind for much of the day. The next day, April 17, the Rebel army resumed its march south before daylight. When the sun rose, the Texans discovered that Canby's army was marching with them, keeping pace on the other side of the river. A Rebel soldier remembered that "the novel spectacle was here exposed of two hostile armies marching side by side down on opposite sides of the same river and in full view of each other."

This continued all day. When one army halted, the other did also. It appeared to another soldier that "neither seeming anxious to bring on a battle," they kept cautious company. Skirmishers occasionally exchanged lead compliments at extreme range. Joe Bowers, an Arizona Guard

The retreat of the Army of New Mexico.

serving with the San Elizario Company, decided that he would find out what the Yankees were up to. So he walked down to the riverbank and yelled across, "Say, I want to know whether you fellows have gone crazy or whether you are a set of damn fools naturally." The Yankees responded with a few shots, which seemed to satisfy his curiosity. Bowers hurried back to his own men without a definitive answer.

By midday, Sibley knew that his plan to outrun Canby's army and overwhelm the Fort Craig garrison was impossible. The Federal army could move faster than Sibley's men. Ahead of them lay a narrow passage at Polvadera and the Fort Craig bottleneck, where they could be trapped. Once more it was time for the Army of New Mexico to choose between unpleasant alternatives. Sibley called a council of war, which soon became heated and passionate, while around the debating officers "the men lounged about seemingly indifferent as to the course the leaders concluded to adopt." The choices were bleak. They were unable to outrun their pursuing enemies and couldn't fight because there were only twenty rounds left for each of the nine remaining artillery pieces and forty rounds of rifle ammunition per man. Finally, a way out of their impasse was offered by some "practical officers," Colonels Green and Scurry, to accept Bethel Coopwood's offer to guide the army around the San Mateo Mountains bypassing Polvadera and Fort Craig. It was a rugged, mountainous, roadless and nearly waterless route that was 108 miles in length. The army would be unable to take its wagons, meaning that they could take with them only what they could carry, and most of the army was now on foot. The decision, once made, was quickly implemented. The men were "ordered to destroy everything but one suit of clothes and prepare seven days rations." All of the wagons but three were abandoned. But the artillery was taken. Scurry pledged that he would get the guns through the mountains somehow. In the late afternoon and evening of April 17, the battered Army of New Mexico turned west, away from the Rio Grande, and began its laborious trek across the untracked wilderness.

The Rebel army was guided by Bethel Coopwood, who had passed along this route when he rejoined the army at Albuquerque after recovering from a near fatal case of measles in Mesilla. He and some San

The San Mateo Mountains, 2011.

Elizario scouts who had accompanied him swung west of the mountains to avoid Fort Craig. Coopwood was aided by a company of native scouts described by one diarist, in error, as "Aragon's men." No other record, official or otherwise, indicates the existence of "Aragon's men." They were presumably Pablo C. Alderete's men. The *Official Records* show that Alderete's company was with the Army of New Mexico both before and after the detour around the San Mateo Mountains. Alderete had also lived nearby in Socorro. They led the army into a rugged, mountainous region, where the water resources were simply inadequate for the number of men and animals trying to pass through.

The next week was an unrelieved hell for the men of the Army of New Mexico and worse for their animals. Day after weary day, they toiled up and down mountain slopes, with little food or water. As they went, they abandoned most of the things they still had with them, including the three remaining wagons and three small cannons, which were buried along with some ammunition. True to Scurry's pledge, the other six guns, those

Monticello Canyon on Alamosa Creek.

captured at Valverde (which became famous as the "Valverde Battery"), were dragged by long lines of half-starved men up and down the steep slopes when the starved mules were unable to continue. It produced a more heroic image than even the original capture of the guns in that dramatic charge at Valverde. The army ran almost completely out of food before the trek was over, and sometimes men and animals went nearly two days without water. Yet somehow these tough men finally reached the Alamosa River on April 24. Food, sent from the south, finally reached them there.

Among those who completed the mountain trek was the Brigand William Kirk. He had been badly wounded at Glorieta when he took over an artillery piece, whose crew had been wiped out, and brought the gun back into service. Apparently fearing to be made a prisoner because of his role in the hijacking of the U.S. Army supply train near Pinos Altos in 1861, he opted to leave the hospital and accompany the retreating army. In the retreat from Santa Fe and Albuquerque and around the mountains, his wounded leg became dangerously infected and was amputated. Kirk must have endured incredible suffering in the rough passage. But he survived and continued to serve the CSA until 1865, rising to the rank of major.

By passing through the mountains, Sibley's men had freed themselves from Federal pursuit. At first, Canby was mystified by the Rebels' actions but soon realized that the Confederates were fleeing New Mexico. He continued along the Rio Grande until his army reached Fort Craig. There he stopped. Captain Paddy Graydon's scouts followed the trail of destruction and abandoned goods that marked Sibley's route, confirming for Canby that the Rebels were in full retreat. The Union forces could almost certainly have headed off the Army of New Mexico before it returned to the Rio Grande; Canby chose not to. Most of his men, particularly the Coloradans, scenting blood, were furious. Especially angry was Chivington, who had moved his command to intercept the Rebels at the Alamosa Creek junction with the Rio Grande but had been recalled. But Canby knew that his own men were already on half rations or worse, that there were no more unexploited food sources in New Mexico and that it would be weeks before food could be shipped from the "states" across the Santa Fe Trail.

Even the civilian population faced starvation. The year 1862 proved to be a disastrous year for agriculture in New Mexico as cold, windy weather continued and the Rio Grande overflowed with an all-time record flood, inundating much of New Mexico's cultivated land. There was simply no way that Canby could feed hundreds of Rebels prisoners, which would be the probable outcome of a battle. Although he never openly stated it, it also appears from his other actions that Canby probably saw no point in slaughtering hundreds of young men when he could achieve the same goals without fighting.

The Confederates passed by the bottleneck and moved south, scattering several encampments from Fort Bliss to Doña Ana along the Rio Grande, with advance detachments near Fort Craig. Although they were relieved at not having to fight their way to their comrades, more than one Rebel opined, as did Theophilus Noel, that "he'd rather fight twenty Yankees than to try another of Coopwood's cutoffs."

Chapter 8
Retreat

Active campaigning by the Army of New Mexico effectively ceased after the retreat around the San Mateo's. Soon, they learned of another Union army approaching them from California. The news came from a small Confederate force sent deep into the western part of the territory, today's Arizona. Company A of Baylor's command had been created at the same time as the Brigands. The company was composed entirely of "Arizonians" and was commanded by the twenty-eight-year-old first lieutenant of the Arizona Rangers, Sherrod Hunter. A Tennessean, Hunter's life had been shattered by the death of his beloved young wife in childbirth. Abandoning a prosperous mercantile business, Hunter had drifted along the frontier for years, sometimes working as a teamster, until 1859. Then he and a few others were the first to establish ranches along the Mimbres River, in the heart of Chiricahua Apache country. The settlers fought stubbornly to hold on against the Apaches but were driven out by early 1861. Hunter was in Mesilla when war came. He took part in the Battle of Mesilla and the capture of the Fort Fillmore garrison as a civilian and then joined the Arizona Guards and was immediately elected first lieutenant.

Hunter's command numbered 54 men when they left the Rio Grande for Tucson on February 1862 in the face of bitter winter weather. One man died of pneumonia, and the others suffered from the cold, but

THE CONFEDERATE TERRITORY OF ARIZONA

The Confederate Territory of Arizona.

the weather probably prevented the Apaches from attacking them. By this point, Arizona's white settlements were tiny specks holding out in the face of Apache hostility. The two mining camps near the Mexican border were soon abandoned, leaving only Tucson. There, the residents greeted Company A with delirious joy as protectors from the Apaches. Their assigned duty, however, was to try to make contact with the supposedly large and vibrant Confederate underground in California and to watch for a large Union army rumored to be coming from that direction. Hunter's orders gave him full latitude and authority to deal with very trying conditions: he had only 74 men, including those who joined in Tucson; was 240 miles from the nearest civilization; was awash in a sea of fierce Apaches; and was awaiting a Union army that numbered 2,300 men.

From Tucson, Hunter led most his company west to see what the Yankees were up to. At the abandoned stage stations and at the Pima and Maricopa Indian Agencies, they found that the Federal troops had been stockpiling grain (one hundred tons), mostly purchased from the Indians, and hundreds of tons of hay in preparation for their invasion of Arizona. At the trading post of Ammi White, a New Englander who served as a lookout for the Yankees and who collected hay and grain for them, they captured a nine-man Union patrol on March 7. Captain James McCleave—a former dragoon master sergeant and General James Carleton's favorite protégé and who also commanded the patrol—was totally surprised to encounter Rebels and was captured without a fight. Carleton, who commanded the "California Column" heading toward Tucson, soon made strenuous efforts to recapture McCleave.

Hunter's men rode farther west, burning the hay stockpiles as they went. At Stanwix Station, only eighty-nine miles from the Colorado River, they exchanged fire with a Union picket on March 29, wounding one man slightly. Hunter then returned to Tucson, leaving a scouting party of ten men to watch for the approaching Yankee column at Picacho Peak, between modern Phoenix and Tucson. Carleton was slow in coming. The Rebels had set back his plans by destroying his feedstuffs, and Carleton, an extremely careful and cautious man, took weeks before he moved again.

In the meantime, the scouts at Picacho Peak had grown bored and careless in the unusually moist and verdant spring weather. When the Yankees did come, they caught the entire patrol, at midday, playing cards in a clearing, with their horses scattered over the hillside, grazing. No sentinels were out, and the first warning Sergeant Henry Holmes and his men had of the presence of the Yankees was when they came bursting into the clearing where they were loafing. Lieutenant James Barrett demanded that the Rebels surrender, which they apparently prepared to do, but then Barrett fired a shot for some reason. Deciding that they were about to be murdered, the Southerners returned fire, hitting seven of the twelve-man Union patrol, three fatally, while no Rebels were hit. All of the Union casualties were hit in the head or upper body. Three Rebels, unable to secure horses, were captured.

The skirmish, the most westerly land combat of the Civil War, has always held a fascination for students of the war. It caused Carleton to fall back again, more than one hundred miles, and it would be another month before he approached Tucson. Before he did, Hunter's little command abandoned the town. They had to fight their way back to Mesilla through the swarming Apaches. On May 4, part of Hunter's men were trapped and nearly annihilated at Dragoon Springs, where at least four men were killed. A party sent in pursuit exacted some vengeance on the Apaches on May 5. To survive, the Rebels armed prisoners, including Captain McCleave, to fight alongside them. The remainder of Company A left Tucson on May 14, and some of the white population went with them back to Mesilla.

The approach of Carleton's California juggernaut finally forced Sibley to take decisive action. For weeks, he and his army had remained passively in their camps scattered from Fort Bliss to above old Fort Thorn. No supplies and no reinforcements came, nor were any coming. None could be obtained locally for lack of specie. Sibley seemed content to passively wait at his headquarters at Fort Bliss. The approach of the California Column and Sibley's inactivity finally caused a near mutiny among Sibley's officers. The officers of the Fifth TMV met in Mesilla on May 12—without their colonel. They listened to reports detailing the condition of the army. The medical officer's report was particularly grim: the army was starving to death. The officers, skirting dangerously close to mutiny, passed a series of cautiously worded resolutions demanding the evacuation of the troops. These were forwarded through channels to Sibley. But copies also went to the governor of Texas, the Confederate secretary of war and to the newspapers. Sibley reacted quickly this time. By late May, the 1,900 soldiers of the army were finally preparing to go home; 600 men under Colonel William Steele were to remain as a rear guard, including all four of the small irregular companies raised in the territory, now temporarily combined into Herbert's Battalion.

Pyron's battalion was the first unit to leave in late May, with Steele's men the last, on the seven-week journey. The tortuous trip homeward was infinitely worse than the trip out. It was now summer and a drought year in the desert. Water was scarce, and the watering holes were easily exhausted. Some watering holes were thirty to forty miles apart. The men were now mostly on foot and weakened by privation and disease. They staggered in small groups across the desert until about 240 miles from San Antonio, when they began to meet civilian relief caravans sent to their rescue. The general consensus of the veterans was that the campaign had been a mistake, their commander was a drunken fool and New Mexico was not fit for human habitation. Behind them, the new Federal troops found New Mexico a more congenial place.

The California Column had originally been formed of California Volunteers by General Edwin V. Sumner in 1861, as part of a planned five-thousand-man force, to go to New Mexico through Mexico, landing at Mazatlan. By the time the force was raised, armed and trained, Sumner had been transferred to the big war in the East, and the Mexicans were having nothing to do with an American army on their soil. Command was passed to Colonel (later General) James Carleton.

A stern, detail-oriented, imperious New Englander, Carlton had seen long service in the First Dragoon Regiment in New Mexico. His command numbered 2,350 men, including the ten companies of both the First and Fifth California Volunteer Infantry Regiments, a company of California Volunteer Cavalry, a battery of Regular artillery (light artillery) and Thompson's howitzer battery of California Volunteers. It was surprisingly deficient in cavalry, but the First California Cavalry had already made an incredible journey by sea to New York so that it could make a symbolic contribution to the Union cause by fighting in Virginia and was not available. To support the movement of the column, Carleton had amassed hundreds of wagons and civilian teamsters to carry the huge quantities of supplies he needed. The force was well trained and well equipped when it left for New Mexico. But it was also far too late in getting there to have any significant effect on the campaign. Carleton had been shocked and delayed by the resistance of Sherrod Hunter's little company, but even without its existence, his arrival would have been too late.

The cautious Federals did not reach Tucson until May 20. There they delayed another month. A three-man party was sent on June 15, mounted on mules, to slip through Confederate scouts and make contact with General Canby's forces at Fort Craig. It consisted of expressman John W. Jones, Sergeant William Wheeling and a guide known as "Chaves." They were jumped by Apaches at Apache Pass on June 18. By abandoning the wounded Chaves, the other two men escaped, but

Wheeling was soon killed and the entire band chased after Jones on his mule. The Indians seemed to enjoy the chase, shouting, "Mucha buena mula," and, "Mucho bravo Americano." Jones finally lost them, and traveling by night and hiding, he finally reached the Rio Grande. There he fell into an exhausted sleep and was only awakened with difficulty by a Confederate patrol that found him and that was very, very interested in his dispatches.

Thus, Colonel William Steele learned before General Canby that the California Column was coming. Incredibly, Canby had never been told by higher headquarters that reinforcements were coming and, at first, refused to believe the reports of contact between Chivington's men on the Rio Grande and the California Column. Steele believed it, and the last of his men, Herbert's battalion of westerners, now headed for San Antonio. For weeks they had been almost without food, and their efforts to impress foodstuffs from the natives had resulted in several pitched battles—which the Rebels did not always win. Behind them they left sick and wounded in Franklin (El Paso). What little hard money Sibley and Steele could raise was left to support them. Some of it was raised by selling surplus munitions to the Mexicans. Later, it turned out that some of the small cannons sold by the Rebels had actually been captured from Union forces. There was a great deal of outrage and a lot of diplomatic correspondence later on the part of the Federal authorities, but nothing came of it. It was the end of August 1862, before the last of Steele's men reached San Antonio. "Starved out, not run out," one veteran insisted.

Chapter 9
After the Rebels

Throughout the remainder of 1862 and 1863, Federal authorities remained alert for a renewal of the Confederate invasion. They were particularly alarmed by the creation of a new regiment under Colonel John Baylor, which was to be recruited from expatriate westerners in exile in Texas. Later this was expanded to an entire brigade, the Arizona Brigade. There were not enough westerners to fill out the four regiments, and they were filled with Texans. The brigade saw service in the Louisiana campaign of 1863 on the frontier fighting Indians, in the Galveston area and in the Red River and Arkansas campaigns of 1864, where it saw heavy combat. It took part in the last land battle of the Civil War, at Palmetto Ranch. The brigade was regarded as the best of the cavalry units in the Trans-Mississippi Department. But it never returned to the New Mexico Territory. The brigade's emotional centerpiece, the "Valverde Battery," came to be regarded as something close to sacred icons by the veterans of Sibley's command. Legend says that the guns were never surrendered but rather were secreted throughout Texas in 1865, with others turned in to the unsuspecting Yankees. Gradually, they emerged from hiding to take their places on various courthouse lawns in Texas as the years passed.

The Fourth Regiment (Baird/Showalter's) was small but was composed mostly of westerners, including a lot of Californians. At the end of the war, the Fourth, serving on the frontier, mutinied. Refusing to surrender, it headed toward New Mexico to raid and continue the war. Loyal Confederate units had to be sent to arrest them. The Third Regiment was commanded by George T. Madison of (modern) Arizona and earned an impressive war record. Madison had replaced Phillips as commander of the Brigands in April 1862. Phillips was killed in an impromptu duel over a card game by Captain Sherrod Hunter after the army returned to Texas. When the army returned to San Antonio, Madison led his thirty-five men north in May 1862, six hundred miles behind Union lines, to rendezvous with Confederate recruits (six hundred to one thousand men) secretly being massed in the mountains of southern Colorado. Union forces broke up the effort, but it was October 1862 before Madison, his men and some recruits reached San Antonio. Pablo C. Alderete retreated to San Antonio with the army but returned on a secret mission to New Mexico at least once. He later rose to command a battalion in Benavide's Texas Cavalry Regiment and, still later, became a wealthy rancher and politician in San Angelo.

Union cavalry cautiously followed the path of the homeward bound Confederates as far as Fort Davis, which they reached on August 12, 1862. The buildings had been stripped, burned and abandoned. For the remainder of the war, the Confederates were content to send occasional scouting parties as far west as the Pecos River to watch for any Federal incursions. Similarly, the Yankees regularly sent patrols as far east as the Pecos. The hostile scouts sometimes found signs of the other side's patrols, but they never again made contact.

In San Antonio, there was also a government in waiting for the Confederate Territory of Arizona, including a governor, territorial secretary and chief justice who never got to go home again. Around these exiles swirled numerous plots and schemes for conquest and clandestine operations that reached into California, Arizona and New Mexico. Of these operations little is known. Captain Henry Kennedy led a clandestine mission to California and Virginia City, Nevada, in 1864 for mysterious reasons. They also made contact with a secret group in (modern) Arizona, fighting a prolonged battle with Apaches in the process. The escort for Kennedy was drawn from John Jarette's company of Quantrill's guerrillas then in Texas and may have included both Cole Younger and

Jesse James, who later claimed that they went. Younger probably did. On their way home from California, Kennedy's men were worsted in a running battle with a band of one hundred mysterious renegades near the Rio Grande, who have never been identified. These secret Rebels passed to and fro through Mexico, and Southern agents maintained permanent bases there, slipping back into Arizona, California and New Mexico. Recruits passed through the network heading east. There was a large nest of Rebels around El Paso and Chihuahua City. It never posed a serious threat to Union control, but it worried General James Carleton and deeply offended his sense of order.

Carleton succeeded to command in the late summer of 1862 when General Canby was ordered east. The crisis had clearly passed. The Colorado troops were ordered home in late July 1862. Canby had already refused reinforcements from Kansas offered by Washington whom he didn't need and couldn't feed. Carleton now faced the problem of preparing for a possible renewed Confederate invasion while taking the field for the long-delayed pacification campaigns against the Apaches and Navajos.

General Canby had already set in motion the basic strategy: deal with the Mescalero Apaches first. There were fewer Apaches, and they were located in the southern part of the territory, where most of the troops already were. This would also allow the Union commanders to keep an eye on possible invasion routes from Texas and have their troops nearby. Therefore, in October 1862, Colonel Kit Carson and the First New Mexico Volunteers returned to ruined Fort Stanton and began combing the White and Sacramento Mountains for hostiles. In November 1862, a column of California and New Mexico Volunteers commanded by Major William McCleave penetrated the Apache stronghold of Dog Canyon in the Sacramento Mountains and caught a large body of Apaches by surprise. Raids like this and incessant pressure prevented the Mescaleros from raiding, gathering food or even resting and destroyed their food supplies and household equipment. The troops were successful in forcing most (425) of the Mescalero Apaches to surrender by the summer of 1863. Campaigning against the remaining renegades continued for seventeen years after the war.

Gradually, Carleton and the territorial authorities became aware that a much bigger war had begun with the Apaches west of the Rio Grande. These western tribes (Chiricahua, Gila, Mimbres, Warm Springs, White Mountain, Coyoteros and others) were several times more numerous than the Mescaleros; were even more warlike, mobile and capable; and lived in an even more rugged land. The war, which flared to a conflagration in 1860 and 1861, heated up even more as it was fed by the Bascom affair at Apache Pass and the attack on Pinos Altos in 1861. In 1862, the great Mimbres Apache leader Mangas Coloradas was captured under a flag of truce and murdered by California troopers at the old Fort McLane site. Shortly thereafter, gold was discovered in central Arizona by an exploring party headed by the old mountain man Joseph Reddeford Walker. The gold rush that followed brought in hundreds of gold seekers and worsened the Indian-white conflict. In 1863, Congress created a new territory, Arizona, with its capital at Fort Goodwin (Prescott). As settlement spread, the war with the western Apaches took on a life of its own and would not end until 1890.

The Navajos posed the biggest problem for Carleton. Mutual raids and reprisals had marked the relationships of the Hispano settlers and the Pueblo Indians on one side and the Navajos on the other for centuries. The U.S. Army had inherited the problem of protecting the settlements from the Navajos at the end of the Mexican-American War. A short period of (relative) peace had ended in August 1861 in a fight over a disputed horse race. Navajo raids had increased in frequency and ranged ever deeper into settled lands in 1862, without Federal soldiers available to intervene. With the Mescaleros under control, Carleton now turned his attention to the Navajos.

Carleton had campaigned several times against the Navajos before 1861, and ever the perfectionist, he was determined to end their menace once and for all. First, he had to break their military will. To do this, he turned again to Kit Carson, the great frontiersman. Carson didn't want the command and tried to resign but was prevailed upon by the imperious Carleton. Carson had developed a dangerous aneurysm near his heart after he was thrown by a horse and longed to spend his last years with his young wife and family in Taos. In the winter of 1863–64, Carson's blue-coated columns ranged throughout the Navajo country, destroying food supplies, clothing, homes and flocks of sheep and capturing herds of horses and mules. They penetrated deep into the Navajo heartland, devastating even the great and mysterious Canon de Chelly. They rarely caught any Navajos but rather forced them to either surrender or starve.

The next step, one Carleton had long planned, was to turn the pastoral and warlike Navajos into settled agrarians. To this end, their flocks and horses were taken from them, and they were taken 240 miles from their homeland to the Bosque Redondo, a forested area, along the Pecos River in the Plains. This was the historic and tragic "Long Walk" of the Navajo people that killed so many in the bitter weather or through starvation. En route, many women and children were kidnapped by Hispanic New Mexicans, to be used as slaves. From the beginning, Carleton's scheme went horribly wrong. Initially expecting about two thousand Indian captives, the army simply could not feed the nearly eight thousand it found. There was no way that food could be moved from the East over the Santa Fe Trail quickly enough to prevent starvation even if Congress had appropriated money to purchase it, which it hadn't. But Carleton was not a man to admit error, and he stubbornly persisted in his scheme. His plans came completely undone when crops failed in 1864 and 1865 and a Congressional investigation uncovered the disaster. By then, all of the Apaches and many of the Navajos had slipped away from the reservation to return to their homelands. Eventually, the government established reservations for both tribes in their original homelands.

Sizeable Union forces were required to keep open the lifeline of the territory, the Santa Fe Trail, stretching back to eastern Kansas. New forts and garrisons were established along the route from Fort Union to Fort Leavenworth. Troops from Kansas and New Mexico, as well as Colorado-based units, patrolled the lengthy trail, which was under frequent attack by Cheyenne and Sioux warriors from the north and the ever deadly Comanches and Kiowas of the Southern Plains. In reprisal to Kiowa and Comanche raids, Carleton sent Kit Carson deep into their Staked Plains homeland in 1864. Carson's force was composed of half infantry, under Lieutenant Colonel Francisco Abreau, and half cavalry, commanded by Major James McCleave; it was accompanied, upon Carson's insistence, by two twelve-pound howitzers. The column left newly built Fort Bascom on November 12 and traveled slowly eastward into the Staked Plains for twelve days.

On the afternoon of the twenty-fourth, Carson's Indian scouts reported a winter encampment in the valley of the Canadian River, thirty miles ahead. After marching all night, the soldiers fell by surprise on the village, destroyed it and captured the horse herd. Then they pressed on to the abandoned Bent and St. Vrain Trading Post known as "Adobe Walls." This is located in modern Hutchison County, Texas, in the Texas Panhandle. From a small mound nearby, where he sited his artillery, Carson could see huge Indian encampments stretching down the Canadian where clouds of warriors were swarming. Sheltered by the old walls and covered by the howitzers, Carson's men were able to fight off the one thousand warriors who attacked them and who were steadily being reinforced. By dark, there were three to four thousand painted warriors surrounding the soldiers.

Deciding that enough was enough, Carson sortied out long enough to destroy another village and then fought his way out of the trap on November 26, 1864. Carson's men had participated in probably the largest battle ever fought with Indians. It had taken all of Carson's considerable skill and the disciplined effectiveness of his soldiers, New Mexico and California Volunteers, to get his command out alive. The two howitzers he had with him had presented a tactical problem for the Indians that they could not solve when combined with his disciplined troops. Carson had been unable to break the Kiowas and Comanches, and he privately admitted his defeat, but smallpox did the job in later years.

With major Indian campaigns in every direction, Union officials were hard-pressed to provide enough troops. The New Mexico Volunteers continued to see extensive service throughout the war and afterward. They became increasingly professional, and the same volunteers and militia who had wilted when facing the Texans proved to be efficient Indian fighters. In 1864, Carleton's command faced a severe manpower shortage when the enlistments of the California Volunteers ran out. To compensate, troops were brought from the East, where the war was obviously winding down. These included the first black troops ever seen in the Southwest. In 1865, the 57th Regiment USCT (U.S. Colored Troops) was marched across the plains from Arkansas, and its companies were distributed as garrisons among several forts. It was later replaced by troops of the 125th USCT.

General Carleton was hard-pressed to feed the men and animals still under his command. Food supplies, particularly fodder for the horses and mules, were not available in sufficient quantities in the territory to meet the needs of the military—or civilians. Enough flour, beans and corn was obtained from Mexico to avert disaster, but the inadequate quality and quantity of food resulted in widespread malnutrition. Even beef was in short supply. It was the army's horses and mules it depended on for mobility that suffered the worst. The Quartermaster Department was simply unable to get enough feed (usually corn) or hay across the Santa Fe Trail from Kansas, from local sources or from Mexico to keep the animals healthy or even alive. As a result, the army was seriously handicapped in its operations. In 1864, for example, Captain William Brady of the California Volunteers was in command of Fort Stanton. He was ordered by General Carleton to take the field with almost all of his small command to chase some Apache renegades. Brady responded respectfully, telling the general that he didn't have any healthy horses. Carleton ordered him out anyway. So Brady and his men dutifully set forth into the White Mountains, on foot, chasing Apaches. Carleton finally relented, realizing the futility of the effort. Brady would later become famous when, as sheriff of Lincoln County in March 1878, he was ambushed and killed by Billy the Kid.

Fearful of a renewed Confederate invasion, and of the mostly imaginary bands of pro-Southerners still lurking in and around the territory, Carleton created a police state in New Mexico. Martial law was maintained throughout the war, although there was clearly no need for it. All mail entering or leaving the territory was inspected and read, and much was secretly copied. No one could enter or leave the territory without the written permission of Carleton's headquarters, and careful records were kept of everyone's movements. Secret informers were everywhere, and many people were arbitrarily arrested for suspicion of being sympathetic to the South and held indefinitely without trial. Even to travel within the territory one had to possess a passport issued by Carleton's office. This latter restriction brought Carleton into bitter conflict with the territorial judges who fought to remove themselves from the strictures of the regulation but paid no attention to other citizen's similar rights. All newspapers were censored, and only approved (Republican) papers were allowed to be sent by mail into the territory.

Many prominent pro-Southerners and all of the Brigands were indicted for treason, and their often considerable property was confiscated. The treason charges were quietly dropped in 1866, but the property was never recovered. Much of it seems to have ended up in the hands of the rapacious Radical Republican legal authorities, Judge Joab Houghton and territorial attorney Abraham Cutler. In southern New Mexico and Arizona, Carleton imposed taxes on things he didn't approve of—Southerners, saloons, gambling establishments and so on—and used the money for things he did approve of: soldiers' relief and pro-Northern newspapers, for example. These are extreme violations of the U.S. Constitution and its laws, and some of his worst excesses were overruled by the U.S. Army adjutant general after repeated complaints reached Washington. By 1865, the New Mexico Territory, on the whole, had had enough of General James Carleton, even though he had dismantled the system of controls by the war's end. The demands for his replacement eventually proved irresistible, and he returned to California, where he had to face a long series of court trials involving rich mining properties that he had ordered confiscated in Arizona that had somehow fallen into private hands.

Epilogue

The quixotic Confederate invasion of New Mexico has sometimes been seen as one of the great what-might-have-beens of this tragic war. If only Sibley had succeeded in carrying through his dreams, New Mexico would have fallen, and then the potential was unlimited. Colorado and California, with their gold that fueled Lincoln's war, would fall, and this could have secured the success of the Confederacy. Or so this imagined alternative to reality goes. On the other hand, the Northern victory has also been celebrated as one of the turning points of this immense struggle. Glorieta has even been described as the "Gettysburg of the West."

Reality is different. Even had New Mexico fallen, simple calculations of numbers, resources and distance would indicate that the North would have held both California and Colorado. The forces, Regular and volunteer, that the Union could call on in the mountain territories and the West Coast were strong enough to resist any probable Confederate incursion. They could also be reinforced more quickly from larger resource reservoirs. If Sibley had been unable to feed his men and horses in New Mexico, it is impossible to imagine how he could have accomplished it over another seven hundred miles of Arizona desert to California or to Colorado. The New Mexico campaign was fought a long way from any vital strategic or political center and was almost unknown to the larger world at the time. It is difficult to sustain the claim that the reasonably possible results of the campaign were, or could have been, decisive for either side. It was a sideshow, albeit an exotic and exciting one. It is far more reasonable to imagine how the world might have changed, had Confederate general Earl van Dorn had another brigade of excellent Texas cavalry at the Battle of Pea Ridge in 1862 instead of at Valverde.

The Civil War in New Mexico did produce some of the most dramatic scenes of the war. The colorful legacy includes the charge of the Lancers and the capture of the "Valverde Battery," the heroic march of the First Colorado Volunteers, the retreat around the San Mateo Mountains, the lonely battle at Picacho and Mrs. Canby's saintly character. It was almost unique in being a three-sided war, with each major combatant also having to fight separate wars with several wild Indian tribes at the same time. The campaign took place on a romantic, distant frontier in a high desert. It was fought in the midst of a newly acquired alien population who had little interest in the outcome. Both sides had to operate nearly one thousand miles from their bases of supply. The scale was small, by the standards of the war—essentially a brigade-sized force fighting a division-sized one. It involved the incredible heroism and tactical skill of the Texas Volunteers and the ineptitude of their commander. The other side was marked by the hard fighting and indiscipline of the Colorado Volunteers and the cool shrewdness of their commander.

Long after the campaign's end, a Union staff officer summed up what made it most unique. The campaign in New Mexico, he wrote, "is unparalleled in history in that while the victorious [Union] Army was tactically defeated in every engagement of any importance, its enemy was finally driven from the invaded territory utterly defeated, disheartened and decimated."

For Further Reading

The quotations throughout are all from the original sources—the various official records, ORs, diaries, letters and so on. Following are sources of further explication.

Alberts, Don E. *The Battle of Glorieta: Union Victory in the West.* College Station: Texas A&M University Press, 1998.

Edrington, Thomas S., and John Taylor. *The Battle of Glorieta Pass: A Gettysburg in the West, March 26–28, 1862.* Albuquerque: University of New Mexico Press, 1998.

Frazier, Donald S. *Blood and Treasure: Confederate Empire in the Southwest.* College Station: Texas A&M University Press, 1995.

Hall, Martin Hardwicke. *The Confederate Army of New Mexico.* Austin, TX: Presidial Press, 1978.

————. *Sibley's New Mexico Campaign.* Albuquerque: University of New Mexico Press, 1960.

Healey, Donald W. *The Road to Glorieta: A Confederate Army Marches through New Mexico.* Bowie, MD: Heritage Books, 2003.

Kelly, Lawrence. *Navajo Roundup*. Boulder, CO: Pruett Publishing Company, 1970.

Masich, Andrew E. *The Civil War in Arizona: The Story of the California Volunteers, 1861–1865*. Norman: University of Oklahoma Press, 2006.

Sabin, Edwin S. *Kit Carson Days, 1809–1868*. 2 vols. Lincoln: University of Nebraska Press, 1995.

Taylor, John. *Bloody Valverde: A Civil War Battle on the Rio Grande, February 21, 1862*. Albuquerque: University of New Mexico Press, 1995.

Thompson, Jerry. *Confederate General of the West, Henry Hopkins Sibley*. College Station: Texas A&M University Press, 1996.

Index

About the Author

D r. Pittman is a retired college history professor and the author of five books—including *Richmond P. Hobson, Progressive Crusader* and *United States Special Operations in the Gulf War*—and seventy-nine articles and papers. He is president of the Boots and Saddles Foundation, past president of Fort Stanton Inc. and on the board of directors of the Lincoln County Historical Society and the New Mexico Military History Society. He earned six college degrees in history, chemistry-physics and geology and served in the U.S. Army, Navy and Air Force (active and reserve), retiring as a lieutenant colonel from U.S. Special Operations Command. He lives in Roswell, New Mexico, with his wife, Kathleen, in a historic restored adobe house.

Visit us at
www.historypress.net